A NATURAL HISTORY OF THE CUCKMERE VALLEY

A NATURAL HISTORY OF THE CUCKMERE VALLEY

Patrick Coulcher

The Book Guild Ltd
Lewes, England

The Book Guild Ltd
25 High Street,
Lewes, Sussex

First published 1997
Reprinted 1997
© Patrick Coulcher, 1997
Set in Times
Typesetting by Acorn Bookwork, Salisbury, Wiltshire

Printed in Great Britain by
Bookcraft (Bath) Ltd, Avon

A catalogue record for this book is
available from the British Library

ISBN 1 85776 158 8

*To my wife Margaret, for her patience,
encouragement and understanding,
and to my mother and sister Susan who also
share my love of the Cuckmere Valley*

CONTENTS

LIST OF ILLUSTRATIONS

FOREWORD
by The Right Honourable Lord Healey of Riddlesden, CH, MBE

It was the beauty of the landscape which first led me to choose the Cuckmere Valley as my home. The wooded hills and sheep-studded meadows reminded me of my native Yorkshire dales, particularly since in places the grass was tawny and patched with gorse and heather. Above all there was the great dome of sky arching over the whole valley from the Weald to the Channel. From my childhood on Ilkley Moor I have always preferred to live on a hill.

The Cuckmere landscape attracts me even more as I grow older. Week by week throughout the year the seasons unfold new beauties. Snowdrops, violets, cowslips, primroses and daffodils announce the spring; bluebells and wood anemones herald the summer. Swallows gather on our rooftop to warn of autumn. Meanwhile the colour of the woods is changing too – from delicate translucent brown, through light green to the darker green of midsummer, and then the final glory of bronze, yellow and scarlet, 'when nature's got her tragic buskin on, and all the rants a mirror of my mood'.

Learning a little of the history of the valley, I have begun to realise how much of the landscape is the product of its history, and how its appearance has changed since mammoths roamed at Arlington. Successive waves of invaders from Central Europe, Italy, Scandinavia and France all left their distinctive mark – above all in a greater density of population than there is today. Even after the invasions ended there were continual changes. Forests were destroyed to fuel the iron furnaces, then replanted to protect Eastbourne's water. Less than 200 years ago ships could sail up to the quays at Alfriston, and smuggling became a thriving trade.

Yet it is only since reading this fascinating book that I have realised the true richness of the Cuckmere Valley in natural life – changing again with the landscape from the marshes round the estuary, the watermeadows higher up, the woods, hills and heathland surrounding the valley, and the Weald beyond.

Patrick Coulcher has done us all an invaluable service by the care and enthusiasm which makes his book a delight to read.

Denis Healey

INTRODUCTION

I first remember seeing the Cuckmere River on a bright sunny spring day in 1947. I was 10 years old and was with my parents on the train from Brighton to Eastbourne. Passing the view of Mount Caburn to my left and the broad sweep of the Downs culminating in Firle Beacon on my right, we soon came to the valley of the Cuckmere, which the railway crossed just north of Sherman Bridge. What attractions this had for me: marsh, woodland, valley, stream and chalk down, all to be explored with the excitement of a boyish mind. This I did, and in my school holidays I could be found, camera in hand, photographing and writing notes on the wildlife of this beautiful valley.

After I left school, the need to follow a career took me far away from the Cuckmere I loved in my youth. It was not until I returned from my chosen profession in early 1992 that my love for this delightful river resurfaced.

The book starts with a brief history of man in the Cuckmere Valley, which sets the scene for the more detailed natural history to follow. I have selected 11 areas within or close by the valley, most of which are little known, quiet and with their own beauty and interesting natural history.

For the purposes of this book the Cuckmere Valley is defined as that part of the river south-west of Hailsham, as north of that town the river divides into smaller tributaries with headwaters in the upper Weald. These tributaries have their own unique natural history, and who knows, if this book proves successful, another could be written.

The reader is invited to explore these areas at leisure and to share the author's excitement at discovering the individual species and points of interest outlined in this book. Exact locations are not often given, so some degree of effort is required of the reader. For the sake of clarity, Latin names of plants have been included in a special section preceding the main index.

This book is not intended to contain a full and precise description of every natural species in the valley; to do so would require an encyclopedia. Nor is it intended for the professional naturalist, although he or she might find something of interest in it. What this book does try to do is to describe some species which have beauty, interest or are peculiar to this area. As such it will appeal to those seeking knowledge about the natural world, and to those who just want to relax, perhaps at home, and read about a lovely part of our British countryside.

A book such as the *AA Book of the British Countryside* will be useful for identifying the butterflies and other insects mentioned in the text. Binoculars and a book such as *The Field Guide to the Birds of Britain and Europe* are essential to learn about and recognise birds. There are many good books to choose from to learn about plants. Perhaps the best for the beginner is W. Keble Martin's *The Concise British Flora in Colour*. Do buy a good hand lens (10 magnification) to examine the detailed structure of plants, and you will not be disappointed by the sheer beauty revealed in the structure and make-up of our wild plants. A map, such as the 1:25000 Ordnance Survey Pathfinder series, numbers 1324 and 1308, will show details of public footpaths and many features not explained in the book. Armed with these few items, the reader will be well equipped to plan and learn from an excursion to any of the areas mentioned.

Please remember at all times to fasten gates, control dogs, guard against fire, leave no litter, keep to public footpaths and protect the plants, trees and wildlife.

I hope that after reading this book the reader will be left with an enquiring mind and a firm resolve to do something positive to help preserve our sadly depleting countryside and heritage.

WARNING: Medicinal properties of some plants and fungi are given in this book. In no circumstances should readers experiment or try these out themselves without sound professional advice.

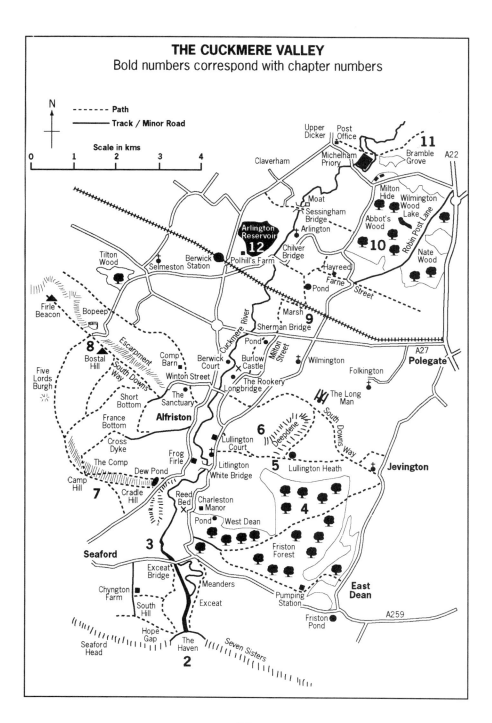

THE CUCKMERE VALLEY
Bold numbers correspond with chapter numbers

N

- - - - Path
———— Track / Minor Road

Scale in kms

0   1   2   3   4

Upper Dicker
Post Office
Claverham
Michelham Priory
11
Bramble Grove
A22

Milton Hide
Wilmington Wood Lake
Moat
Sessingham Bridge
Arlington
Abbot's Wood
Robin Post Lane

Arlington Reservoir
12
Chilver Bridge
10
Nate Wood

Tilton Wood
Berwick Station
Selmeston
Polhill's Farm
Hayreed
Farne Street
Pond

Firle Beacon
Bopeep
Cuckmere River
Marsh
Sherman Bridge
9

Escarpment
Pond
Milton Street
Wilmington
A27
Polegate

Five Lords Burgh
Bostal Hill
8
South Downs Way
Comp Barn
Berwick Court
Burlow Castle
Folkington

Winton Street
The Rookery
Longbridge
The Long Man

Short Bottom
The Sanctuary
Deepdene

France Bottom
Alfriston
6
South Downs Way

Cross Dyke
Lullington Court
Jevington

The Comp
Frog Firle
Litlington
White Bridge
5
Lullington Heath

Camp Hill
7
Dew Pond
Cradle Hill
Reed Bed
Charleston Manor
4

Seaford
3
Pond
West Dean
Friston Forest

Exceat Bridge
Meanders

Chyngton Farm
South Hill
Exceat
Pumping Station
East Dean

Hope Gap
The Haven
Seven Sisters
Friston Pond
A259

Seaford Head
2

XV

1

A HISTORY OF THE CUCKMERE VALLEY

Early Man in the Cuckmere Valley

In the dim and distant past, some 10,000 years ago, Palaeolithic people lived in Sussex. Little is known of their way of life, but their cultures covered a long period of time, representing man's evolution from ape to *Homo sapiens*. They sheltered mainly in caves, and were hunters and food gatherers with a nomadic or semi-nomadic existence, moving on when local food supplies ran out or to follow migrating animals. Few signs of their existence have been found, but well-made Palaeolithic hand axes and tools have been discovered in various sites in the Cuckmere Valley such as Exceat, West Dean and further north in the river gravel at Arlington.

After the Palaeolithic period came the Mesolithic Age, which lasted from about 8300–4000 BC. The first group of Mesolithic people walked here from the Continent, which at that time was joined with England. The Sussex Downs escaped glaciation, but they must have presented an incredibly bleak appearance with snowdrifts occupying many of the valleys until late in summer. There were few trees, but in low-lying areas bushes and scrub provided food for mammoths and other large animals that roamed the tundra-like Downs. It is interesting to note that during the construction of the reservoir at Arlington in 1969 a mammoth's tusk and other prehistoric animal bones were uncovered. Such plants as the *common rockrose*, found on the open downland, may be survivors from this period of intense cold.

It was not until 5000 BC, when the glacial age rapidly came to an end, that the seas rose and England was severed from the Continent by the formation of the Channel. Where the chalk downs dipped into valleys, they became white cliffs, the best-known being the North Downs at Dover and the South Downs around Beachy Head and westwards.

The population increased in the latter part of the Mesolithic Age owing to climatic change, improved technology and possibly migration by peoples from the Continent who landed on our shores undeterred by the formation of the Channel. Mesolithic people preferred to live on mounds of sandy outcrop, and for hunting they fashioned delicate weapons of flint. At Selmeston, near the Cuckmere, actual Mesolithic dwelling pits were found with ashes of hazelwood fires. Probably the shallow pits were roofed with hazel boughs to provide shelter.

Between 4000 and 3000 BC the first real settlers arrived in Sussex, living on the summits and slopes of the chalk hills where traces of their habitations are most numerous. These Neolithic people, as they were called, found the chalk downland easiest to clear and cultivate. Other areas, such as the Weald to the north and the river valleys, were covered with a jungle of birch, hazel and bog. Few tracks penetrated this dark interior, and it was inhabited by dangerous animals such as the bear, wolf and boar. So Neolithic man inhabited the Downs, existing largely as a cultivator of the soil using primitive tools made of flint and animal horns. They grew corn and were probably the first to domesticate animals, reverting to hunting and fishing when times were hard.

In about 1800 BC Bronze Age people began to arrive, bringing with them superior weapons and implements made of bronze, an alloy of copper and tin. The clearance of the Downs proceeded apace, and small hut villages and even farmsteads were formed. These people introduced primitive ploughing and a complicated field system, a style that lasted for many hundreds of years.

Around 500 BC new invaders from the Continent came to the shores of Sussex. These Celts, as they were called, brought with them a new material, black in colour: iron. These Iron Age Celts were artistic, talented, aggressive and warlike, and they built massive hilltop forts such as that at Seaford Head, now mostly fallen into the sea. Often, these obliterated Neolithic earth mounds already there. They gradually took over from the Bronze Age people; they improved the existing farm methods and established their own tribal system, dividing the chalklands into regions. Evidence of Celtic farming methods can be seen in the shape of terraces on steep downland slopes, and raised banks on more gentle inclines. These 'lynchets', as they are called, are derived from a Saxon word meaning 'little hill'. They are thought to have been formed deliberately by the primitive ploughing of the same furrow year after year and generation after generation. A terraced, level area of deep soil was formed above the surrounding area of shallow earth, so facilitating the planting of crops. Such lynchets can be seen in the form of two large terraces to the east of the Cuckmere at Exceat. Celtic ironsmiths too were adept at making iron jewellery and body ornaments, and also in constructing metal tools for land use.

Each of these different ages did not suddenly begin when one ended, but each fused and overlapped one with another. The Iron Age fused with the Bronze Age, just as the Bronze Age did with the Neolithic, and the Neolithic with the Mesolithic.

Roman Occupation

The Cuckmere appeared to be little affected by the military expeditions of Caesar in 54 and 55 BC. However, the main Roman invasion in AD 43, which lasted in a permanent occupation of 350 years, did have a significant effect visually and economically, as well as culturally.

Iron-working, probably started by the Celts, was increased, and many sites are recorded in the Cuckmere area, notably at Waldron, Heathfield and Warbleton. The Romans were, of course, great road builders, and they are thought to have constructed crossings of the Cuckmere at Exceat, to pioneer a coastal route to Pevensey, and a less exposed route at Chilver Bridge some ten kilometres upriver. This latter route was called Farnestreet, and connected Lewes with the Roman fortress at Pevensey, built in about AD 280. Farnestreet still exists as a deep muddied track, as do Moopshill Lane and Whiteing Lane to the east of Chilver Bridge. Chilver Bridge was known as Chiselford as long ago as 1252, and by 1689 was referred to as Chisselford Bridge. The possible meaning of the word 'Chisselford' being 'pebble or shingle ford'.

Arlington was an important settlement area during the Roman occupation, and it is claimed that a temple existed on the site of the parish church. Roman pottery and the site of a potter's workshop at Polhill's Farm were discovered during the construction of Arlington Reservoir. During the Roman period, the underlying water-table was much higher than it is today, and there were deep creeks and inlets reaching inland along the coast. The Cuckmere was possibly navigable as far as Arlington, and it has been suggested that shipbuilding may have been carried out at this site.

Under the Romans, England prospered. They built large, comfortable villas, and one could imagine well-to-do Britons adopting Roman ways. Their advanced farming methods, including simple ploughs, were used on large estates worked by slaves or serfs. Sussex, with its many ports, would have benefited enormously from the increasing trade with the Continent.

The cultured and colonial style of living created by the Romans lasted until early in the fifth century AD, when hordes of barbarians from the East ransacked Rome, and the Romans left England to protect their homeland. The survivors of their civilisation, the Romano-British, were left to fend for themselves against new invaders from the Continent.

Anglo-Saxon Invasion

Around AD 450 the seas were still rising as the glaciers melted, and the low-lying countries of northern Europe were reducing in size. Thus, there was good reason for these Saxon people, hungry for land, to look to invade a relatively sparsely inhabited England. The South Saxons, who gave the county of Sussex its name, were the most successful in our area. They came in small boats from an area just south of Denmark and raided and pillaged before eventually establishing settlements all along the Cuckmere Valley. One such settlement and burial site at Winton Street in Alfriston was discovered in 1912 by workmen digging the foundations for a new house now called The Sanctuary. Altogether about 120 graves and items were encountered, such as rings, Roman coins, pins, buckles, axe heads, swords and knives, suggesting that trading had been carried out between the Saxons and the Romano-British.

The names of many Cuckmere parishes derive from the language of these Germanic invaders. Some parish names were called after their leaders, such as Sessingham, the water meadow of Seaxa's people, and Lullington, the settlement of the people of Lulla.

The main Saxon invasion, led by Aella, probably took place in the Cuckmere region in about 457, when the Britons were defeated and fled into the forests. *The Anglo-Saxon Chronicle*, a ninth-century document, suggests that some sort of treaty was agreed. This was the Mearcredesburna, which literally means 'the river of the frontier agreed by treaty'. This treaty was broken in 465 when Saxon fought Briton at the battle of Mearcredesburna.

No one is sure where this battle was fought, but the next recorded event was in 471, when Pevensey Castle was besieged and the defenders subsequently slaughtered. The Cuckmere was the only river between the Saxon stronghold above Alfriston and their objective at Pevensey, and it is probable that the Battle of Mearcredesburna was fought along its banks. There were only three crossing points in the area at that time: Chilver Bridge, Milton Street and Exceat. Strategically, it would have suited the Saxons to secure the downland ridge from the east of the Cuckmere to Beachy Head, and therefore Mearcredesburna could have taken place in the area of the old Neolithic fording point opposite Milton Street. No evidence of a battlefield here has yet been unearthed, but who knows what may eventually be discovered?

Saxon people were gradually converted from paganism to Christianity, mainly by the influence of St Wilfrid, an exiled northern bishop who established himself in Sussex in the seventh century. Saxon churches were built, many on sites where their pagan rituals had been carried out. The Saxons continued to clear the Wealden forests (the word 'weald' is derived from the Saxon word 'wold', meaning 'forest') and they farmed the land and established villages.

In the late Saxon period, fortified settlements or burghs (the forerunner of our boroughs) were built to counter Viking marauders from Scandinavia. Despite these defence measures, the Vikings subdued the north of England, and at the beginning of the eleventh century Canute of Denmark became King of England. Seven years after Canute's death in 1035, a Saxon prince, Edward the Confessor, was elected King. King Edward owned a good deal of land in the Cuckmere Valley, comprising three manors at Exceat, two at West Dean and one at Charleston. He also owned Berwick and Claverham and part of Frog Firle on the western side of the river.

So in Anglo-Saxon England, at the end of the first millennium AD, the foundations of much of our present culture and way of life were laid, and although rival chieftains and princes fought and feuded amongst themselves, the seeds of a more stable and prosperous land were being sown. But change lay ahead.

Norman Invasion

The Anglo-Saxon nation was shattered in 1066 after Edward the Confessor died. William, Duke of Normandy – who had been promised the throne of England by Edward but was usurped by one Harold Godwinson (the son of the Earl of Godwin of Wessex) – made preparations to invade, with the blessing of the Pope. He landed at Pevensey, and the subsequent Battle of Hastings resulted in William being crowned King of England on Christmas Day 1066. Sussex and the security of the Channel ports was important to William because of his need to maintain links with Normandy.

William moved fast to secure his kingdom. He gave out large holdings of land in exchange for services and fealty, and most of the Cuckmere manors were given to his trusted companions. Only one of the Saxon ruling class retained his Cuckmere estate, and that was a man called Heming, who kept his manor at Exceat. On the other hand, one Norman lord named Ralph was given Charleston Manor and eight houses in West Dean, both areas where salt-workings existed.

The Normans brought with them from France a new culture and high standards. Their builders, too, were more confident than the Saxons, creating churches and castles which were very sturdy and bold. The Norman influence continued for centuries, but eventually they were integrated into the English nation and their speech was blended into the English language.

After the Normans

The Normans were the last successful invaders of England. One would have thought that their influence would have stabilised and cemented relations with the Continent. But too often in the centuries that followed the Norman invasion England was at war with France, Germany, Holland or Spain. The Hundred Years' War of the fourteenth century was a particularly prolonged period of fighting when the French throne was claimed by Edward III. Both sides made continuous raids on each other, and the Cuckmere area was very vulnerable. By 1356 Seaford was for the most part burned down and devastated by pestilence and the calamities of war.

During the Middle Ages the Downs were converted from arable land to sheep pasture, and the hills would be very much as they are now, haunts of peace with only the sounds of birds and the wind to disturb the tranquillity. Here and there could be seen the first windmills on the hills, and these complemented the watermills on the Cuckmere, which were constructed hundreds of years before by the Romans. Throughout our history economic requirements have led to frequent changes in farming from arable to pasture, and vice versa. At the end of the eighteenth century, demand for grain, created by the Napoleonic Wars, resulted in large areas of downland being ploughed up yet again. The repeal of the Corn Laws in 1846 encouraged many farmers to revert back from arable to grass, and so the chalkdown grasslands increased in size, and many that exist today date back to these changes in the mid-nineteenth century. Imports of cheap wool and mutton from New Zealand towards the end of the 1880s made sheep farming less profitable, and by the time of the First World War sheep numbers on the Downs were down to about a third of their original levels. The reduction in grazing allowed the encroachment of scrub, mainly gorse, elder and bramble, on ancient grasslands.

The need for cereals in the First and Second World Wars resulted in more downland being ploughed, and in 1945 government grants providing subsidies for cereal farming had a disastrous effect on many remaining areas of old chalk grasslands. Cheap artificial fertilisers meant that cereal-growing on even the poorest land became more profitable than rearing sheep. So our chalk grasslands began to disappear except on the steeper slopes which were impractical to plough. Scrub invasion on these remaining grassland slopes continued during the post-war period due to reduced grazing, and the spread of scrub was given a boost in 1953 with the arrival of myxomatosis, which decimated the rabbit population.

The need for nature conservation came into prominence in the 1960s, and such bodies as the Sussex Wildlife Trust have done much to protect what is left of our chalk grassland and the rare flora that co-exists with it. In the lower Cuckmere area the County and District Councils and the National Trust preserve the Seven Sisters and the countryside to the south of Frog Firle. Areas of outstanding chalk grassland can be found at Lullington Heath, Deep Dene and Windover Hill, as well as on the Cuckmere Valley slopes near High-and-Over and at Exceat.

The destruction of the wildwood continued after the Norman invasion as more cultivated land was needed to support an increasing population. As the wildwood was cleared, so the plants and animals that existed in them were able to spread and colonise the open spaces. Until about two centuries ago many of the ancient woodlands were managed under a coppice system, where the underwood was cut on a 7 to 20 year cycle, depending on the species. An example of this can still be seen in the Cuckmere Valley, at Bramble Grove. About 200 years ago plantation forestry became popular, especially on large country estates. Later, as the economic value of such estates was recognised, commercial organisations began to plant extensive tracts of former downland. For example, in the 1920s, Friston Forest was created from sheep pasture in order to protect Eastbourne's water supply.

The extensive water-meadows in the Cuckmere Valley, particularly in its lower reaches, which were once the home to many indigenous plant, bird and animal species, have gradually been drained to meet the needs of the farmer. Only a few small areas of this former habitat are still to be seen, particularly below High-and-Over and near Arlington. South East Water now owns the areas of Arlington Reservoir, Lullington Heath, Deep Dene and Friston Forest, and, with the aid of English Nature and the Forestry Commission, manages them in the interests of nature conservation.

Our brief history of the Cuckmere Valley has shown how man and climatic changes have shaped and moulded the landscape into what we see today. Plant and animal life, although much depleted since former days, still gives us a varied and interesting heritage. This heritage must be protected at all costs from further exploitation and destruction.

Gannet

2

THE CUCKMERE HAVEN

The Cuckmere is a small river; from its many sources in the High Weald to its estuary it is 45 kilometres long, and with its tributaries flows through varied landscapes that are famed for their beauty and natural history. An ancient Saxon name, 'Cuckmere' means 'fast-flowing water'. The Cuckmere has not always been so called, for it has also been known as 'the Wandelmestro', a fitting description of this wandering waterway.

Our first area to explore is the Haven itself, where the Cuckmere flows into the sea. The Cuckmere is the only Sussex river which does not have a port or industrial complex at its mouth. Only a natural beauty prevails here, with the magnificent gleaming white chalk cliffs of the Seven Sisters culminating in Haven Brow, the highest Sister, on the eastern side, and Seaford Head, with its brown tertiary sandstone overlying the chalk, on the western side.

Chalk plays an important part in our story, and a brief description is necessary. The chalk of the South Downs is soft, brilliant white and mostly pure limestone. Some hundred million years ago microscopic creatures with an algae-like appearance drifted in the surface water of the sea, and when they died they deposited crystals of calcite (calcium carbonate) on the sea floor. These accumulated, together with fragments of shells, into a calcareous ooze, which, when compacted, formed the chalk we see today.

Dark bands of flint can be seen at almost regular intervals all the way up the chalk cliffs. Flint, as we have seen from the first chapter, played an important part in the evolution of man in the Cuckmere Valley. Like the chalk, flint has a biological origin and is derived from the skeletons of minute animals called Radiolaria that floated with the algae in ancient seas, and from the tissues of siliceous sponges that lived on the seabed. These animals, in decaying, formed lumps of crystalline silica or flint nodules. Nobody knows for sure why these nodules formed bands, but it is thought that they formed along bedding planes and in the burrows of animals. Another theory has it that the algae and sponges required a certain sea temperature to bloom and flourish, and as the earth's axis tilted back and forth over tens of thousands of years (the Milankovitch effect), the sea temperature rose and fell correspondingly. Thus the flint formed in bands on the seabed according to the temperature fluctuations over the millennia.

If you wander along the shore towards Birling Gap as the tide is receding, you will come across areas where over thousands of years the sea has formed deep gullies through a plane of hard flint by erosion of the soft chalk underneath. In these gullies large pools have formed into which huge boulders have fallen. Look carefully at the edge of these underground boulders, and on a day when the sea is calm and the water is clear and unmuddied you may well see the red feelers of a large *common lobster*. Tickle the edge of the boulder with a long thin stick and you can tempt this great predator of the pool out from his lair. In these deep pools and in the shallower ones further up the beach you will find all sorts of sea life from *sea scorpions* (an abundant harmless little fish common in our rock pools) to *sea anemones* and *shrimps*. You may also be lucky to find heavy lumps of brown mottled rocks which, when broken open, reveal striations of iron, coloured yellow and silver. These pyrite nodules, as they are called, are made up of iron sulphide or 'fool's gold', and have been used in the making of sulphuric acid.

The Haven itself is a shingle beach with a man-made salt marsh lagoon to landward which was constructed in 1975 to attract wading birds. Many years ago, at the end of the last century, the shingle was a suspected nesting site for a pair of *little terns*, now a rare and declining species due to the pressure of too many human visitors. In the 1960s the last colony of little terns ceased to breed on the Crumbles, some 10 kilometres to the east. About 30 years ago the *ringed plover* also nested at the Haven. These birds are

...ll seen frequently on the shingle, and could again be breeding in the area.

How exciting it is that the chalk cliffs again echo to the high chattering 'kek-kek-kek' of the *peregrine falcon*, which has recently returned after an absence of some 33 years. This magnificent bird declined and finally disappeared, mainly because of the effects of pesticides in its prey, such as rabbits and birds. The peregrine nests on ledges high up on the chalk cliffs, where it lays a clutch of three or four richly coloured buff, red and grey blotched eggs. What a great reward to conservation efforts if this bird has indeed returned to build again on the Seven Sisters.

On the Downs on either side of the Haven can often be seen the *wheatear*, the *stonechat*, and of course the *skylark*. Of these, the migrant wheatear has declined greatly since the eighteenth and nineteenth centuries, when shepherds supplemented their wages by catching the birds with nets and specially constructed cages. They sold them for two old pence a brace to the markets in London and Brighton, where they were bought as a great delicacy for the dinner tables of country gentry. Some shepherds caught as many as 80 dozen wheatears in one day. The wheatear generally nests in a rabbit hole, the nest being made of grass and moss with a lining of rabbit's fur, hair, feathers or wool. The first eggs are laid at the end of April, with second clutches in June. The parent bird sits very tight, and almost the only way to find their nest is to watch the female back – and this requires patient watching. Often the male bird accompanies the female back, and a hopeful sign is when they both turn their backs and start a series of 'hops' from perch to perch. The final flight to the nest is sometimes difficult to see and may be some 20 to 30 metres in length. It is easier to watch the birds return when the nest is being built or when the young are hatching.

The male *stonechat*, with its distinct black head and throat and persistent scolding note, 'wheet, tsack, tsack', like hitting two stones together, is often seen on a bramble bush or large grass tussock on the downland slopes near the sea. It makes its nest on or near the ground amongst grass, brambles or at the foot of gorse bushes. The nest, made of roots, grass and moss, with a lining of hair, feathers and fine grass, is hard to find, but the parent birds can be watched back in a similar manner to that described for the wheatear.

The *fulmar petrel* is a relatively new bird to the chalk cliffs of Sussex, having started to breed in small numbers in the late 1960s. The fulmar spends the autumn months out in the open sea, coming back to land in early winter to commence its breeding cycle. In May it lays a single white egg on broad cliff ledges with little or no nest material. Only one clutch is laid, so success is dependent on no predation by rats or larger seabirds such as *herring* and *black-backed gulls*. Its defence mechanism is to spit vile green stomach oil, which has a stinging effect on its predators. The oil can be spat to a distance of as much as three metres.

On the windswept beach on a cold winter's day, when great grey walls of water are pounding and hissing on the shores, you may see a variety of gulls, mainly herring and black-headed, wheeling to and fro over the sea. At the same time, a group of *oyster-catchers* is standing on the shingle bank, cold and forlorn, looking out to sea, contemplating this bleak scene.

The Cuckmere Haven is an exciting place to be during the spring and autumn migrations, when unusual and rare birds can be seen, such as *avocets* and *flamingoes*. The avocet is an unmistakable bird, with its long slender upturned or awl-shaped bill and contrasting black and white plumage. It uses its bill to sweep the shallow water in a side-to-side motion to locate and feed on small shrimps and water insects. The avocet ceased to breed in Britain in about 1843, but returned to form a small colony at Minsmere, Suffolk, in 1947. Since then, thanks to conservation efforts of the RSPB, it now breeds in many places on the east coast.

On the Seven Sisters many beautiful butterflies may be seen, most of which are mentioned in later chapters. However, a special mention here must be made of the *clouded yellow*. This migrant butterfly breeds continuously in North Africa and the Mediterranean, and every spring it migrates north. In most years this migration loses momentum in central France, but exceptionally the clouded yellows reach the British Isles, sometimes in large numbers, such as in 1947, 1955, 1983 and 1992. What a thrill it is to see the fast flying flash of chrome yellow across the open downland. The clouded yellow feeds on the nectar of such common plants as clover, thistle and knapweed. Spring migrants to Britain lay a single clutch of eggs that hatch in autumn. They cannot survive the cold damp weather beyond November, and hence they, like that other migrant, the *painted lady*, attempt a return migration in October, moving back south to warmer lands.

On the Downs above the Haven on sunny days in high summer, you will see the orange brown *gatekeeper* butterfly, or *hedge brown* as it is sometimes known, because it is often seen near country hedgerows. The female lays her eggs singly on grasses; they hatch in about three weeks. The caterpillars feed at night on grasses and they hibernate for the winter while still quite small. They recommence feeding in spring and form a chrysalis in June from which the adult butterfly emerges in July. The gatekeeper feeds on the nectar of brambles and valerian and lives for only about three weeks.

Let us take a look at the steep shingle bank where the white cliff of Haven Brow forms a magnificent backdrop to this coastal vista. The shingle bank was created over thousands of years. The continuous pounding of the waves has washed up the shingle into a bank and left it high and dry. The bank is terraced on the seaward side, and a storm shelf is evident where shingle has been pushed up to a higher level than normal during particularly violent storms.

The vegetation on the top of the bank is relatively sparse and limited to the plants that can tolerate biting cold sea winds and salt spray. Their roots delve deep down to find water and their leaves are adapted to withstand the drying effect of the wind.

In summer, one of the first plants you will notice on the top of the bank is *sea kale*, which forms small rounded bushes of stiff green leaves. A member of the cabbage family, its leaves can be cooked and eaten as a vegetable. The clusters of small white four-petalled flowers appear in July. Later, the seeds are protected in hard globular capsules which can float along the coast intact for many months or years before coming to rest on a new shingle bank. The botanist A.H. Wolley-Dod commented in his *Flora of Sussex* of 1937 that sea kale was rare at Cuckmere Haven. Evidently it has increased since then.

The yellow flowers and grey-green leaves of *yellow horned-poppy* add colour to the shingle bank from June onwards. The plant earns its name from the long horn-like seed capsules which given an architectural symmetry to the plant.

Sea beet colonises the shingle. You can recognise it by its dark green fleshy leaves and its long greenish-yellow flower spikes on the stem and side branches. This plant is closely related to the vegetable we know as spinach beet.

Now probably extinct at the Haven, *sea holly* was recorded as being plentiful in 1851. A single plant was seen in 1935 and in 1978. It is an attractive plant with grey-blue holly-like leaves and pale blue flowers. I wonder why it declined and what conditions it needs to re-establish itself here?

The red, pink and white flowers of *red valerian* splash colour on the stable shingle bank near the river mouth. It is not a native plant, but may have been introduced from a Mediterranean country. It was first noticed growing on walls in Lewes around

1790, and seems only to have arrived at Cuckmere Haven since the Second World War.

Lower down the landward side of the main shingle bank, where protection from the wind is afforded, you will see patches of *stonecrop* and *scentless mayweed*. Where grass has further stabilised the shingle, other plants such as *hound's-tongue*, *bristly ox-tongue* and *smooth hawksbeard* have taken hold.

Much of the level area of shingle behind the bank is covered with *sea couch grass*, but it is also home to other more interesting plants. *Rock sea lavender*, one of the most beautiful flowers of the coast, about 20 centimetres high, bears numerous tiny pale lilac flowers on stiff, forked branches. It flowers from July to September. *Narrow-leaved bird's-foot trefoil*, flowering slightly earlier, forms a mat on the shingly ground. It has longer, more wiry stems and narrower leaflets than its more common counterpart, the *common bird's-foot trefoil*. In August and September look out for the fleshy-looking blue-green leaves and small yellowish flowers of the *rock samphire*. It grows 30 centimetres tall among the plants of the shingle, and is conspicuous because of the contrasting colours of its leaves and flowers. Sadly, it has been exterminated from some areas of our coast because it was extensively collected in Victorian times to make into pickle. Its stems and leaves are also edible when young.

The lagoon below the shingle bank is edged with a short mat of the fleshy bright green stems and leaves of *glasswort*. In autumn, this mat takes on a reddish hue. Bordering the river is a wide expanse of salt marsh, grey-green with the leaves of *sea purslane*, a plant that can tolerate having its roots regularly soaked in sea water at high tide. This is such a successful species that it dominates this habitat to the exclusion of other plants.

On the cliff top just to the east of the Haven, the purple flowers of the *wall germander* may be found growing in August and September on the west facing slope where rabbits and the prevailing winds have rendered the turf short. It is now a few years since the plants were last seen, and as they are only a few centimetres high you will need patience and a good eye to find them. Because of recent cliff falls, some could be close to the cliff edge, but most grow some 15 metres or so inland. Wall germander was grown in Queen Elizabeth I's reign as an aromatic plant for the garden, and as its name suggests it is often found on walls. It used to grow for many years at Camber Castle, near Rye. Sadly, it has now become extinct there. The plant was always thought to have been introduced by man on such walls because in its natural Mediterranean habitats it grows on grassy banks and waste ground. The Cuckmere Haven site is a similar habitat to that on which it grows on the French side of the Channel, and therefore these Cuckmere flowers are almost certainly native plants and not introduced by man. Let us hope that they still remain here and that you will experience the excitement of their discovery. But do not get too close to the cliff edge in your exuberance!

On the western side of the Haven, near South Hill, lies a small nature reserve at Hope Gap, which is certainly worth a visit. It can be approached either from Seaford along the coastal path or from the west side of the Cuckmere Haven. One peculiarity of the site is that for about a metre from the cliff side the turf, already kept short in the area by rabbits, has been stripped bare by the wind sweeping up over the edge. In places the edges have a silver hue with just a hint of blue where the leaves of *buck's-horn plantain* form a mat close to the brown soil. *Thrift*, or *sea pink*, with its woody rootstock and charming pink flower clusters, can be found at almost any time of the year, except winter, giving a contrast of colour to the somewhat barren cliff edge.

In this area in July and August the *henbane* can also be found, growing up to a metre tall, with large pale yellow flowers veined in dark purple, so distinctive that it is not possible to confuse them with those of any other British plant. Henbane, a member of the potato and nightshade family, is extremely poisonous, and all parts of the plant contain a narcotic drug called hyoscine, which is a sedative, analgesic and spasmolytic. Henbane oil can be produced from the leaves, and is used for disorders of the eye and for rheumatism. In some Mediterranean and Asian countries it is still used as an aphrodisiac, and in medieval times it was administered as a love potion – sometimes with disastrous effects. With such properties it is not surprising that for many centuries it was grown in British gardens. A plant used by witches and sorcerers throughout the ages is one to steer very clear of, and should only be handled by experts. Strangely, the plant is usually associated with the disturbed ground around rabbit burrows.

Another, but quite uncommon, plant to be found here in July and August is the *mountain stone parsley*, a member of the carrot family. In this locality it is quite short, but it can grow up to 60 centimetres tall and has strikingly pure white flowers arranged in compact heads. One characteristic of this plant is that its whiteness makes it 'glow' in the dark, and with only a small amount of moonlight it stands out easily from other members of the carrot family with which it grows. This interesting feature probably enables night-flying insects to locate it, and has given the plant the more popular name of *moon carrot*.

On the areas of short turf where the grasses are browned and seared, not only from rabbit activities but also as a result of exposure to salt winds, look out for the *dwarf centaury*. This rare plant is a dwarf form of the *common centaury*, and is only some three centimetres tall. It survives the winter as a ground-hugging rosette of spoon-shaped leaves and produces its five-petalled pink flowers in June to September. The centaury is a valued herb which is collected and dried and taken in tea form to aid digestion, flatulence and heartburn. In August and September you will find the vivid blue flowers of a dwarf form of the *clustered bellflower* growing in the short turf around rabbit burrows. Rabbits seem to avoid the plant, and so it stands out as a splash of colour against its somewhat barren surroundings.

Before leaving this area of Hope Gap, look out to sea, and on a clear day in spring or early summer, when the sea sparkles with the hint of a fine sunny spell to come, you may sometimes see *gannets* plunging headlong into the sea after fish. The nearest breeding colony is on Alderney in the Channel Islands, and these birds have possibly flown from there. What a magnificent sight they are, and once seen never forgotten.

Around and to landward of Hope Gap lies an area of bush and scrubland where every year thousands of migrating birds pause on their outward journey. They feast on the berries and other food here before setting off in large flocks across the Channel to far-off lands in southern Europe and Africa. This site is one of many staging posts in the area, and when springtime arrives to herald warmer weather, so the birds return to rest and catch the first insects before proceeding inland to their summer breeding territories. For thousands of years their ancestors have undertaken the same dangerous journeys over hundreds of miles of sea, land and desert. Migration is one of the wonders of the natural world, and as we gaze upon the thousands of birds wheeling and diving around the chalk cliffs of Hope Gap we can only wonder as to what instinct or memory drives them to find the same spot year after year.

This chapter has given only a brief description of some of the natural life that can be seen around the Haven, a place where indeed the waves break loud on the seashore; and the reader is invited to make a closer inspection to discover the many other interesting species which have not been included.

16

3

THE MEANDERS AND EXCEAT BRIDGE
TO LITLINGTON

Before 1846 the Cuckmere wound itself through a series of horseshoe bends from Exceat Bridge to the sea. This distinctive flow pattern was called 'the Meanders', after the River Menderes in Turkey. The Cuckmere Meanders before the mid-eighteenth century used to flood and silt up, caused by the phenomenon of longshore drift. This phenomenon is the tendency for shingle to be piled up by the prevailing wind and tide, and in the Cuckmere's case this meant a continual shifting of the river mouth to the east towards the Seven Sisters. Eventually, because of the cliffs, the entrance was blocked, ships could not enter the mouth and serious flooding was caused upstream. So in 1846 a straight cut was made to bypass the Meanders below Exceat Bridge, and the outfall of the river was maintained in its present position by securing the banks with vertical planks. The effect of longshore drift was reduced with the construction of a concrete sea wall on the Seaford side.

The bridge at Exceat has an ancient origin, and a causeway probably existed there before Romano-British times. A succession of wooden bridges was probably started here by the Romans, but it was not until 1656 that a stone bridge was built, and this was considered sufficiently important to be recorded in the East Dean church register. To the east of the bridge was a narrow raised causeway, just wide enough to take a horse and carriage. In fog or at night it was a dangerous route, and in about 1810 a wagon overturned, tipping its 18 occupants and horses down the south bank. Luckily, all were uninjured, but following a similar incident a few years later, when a lady was killed, the causeway was widened by taking much of the topsoil and rubble and extending the northern side. The southern edge was left at its original height, probably to prevent the inundation of the sea. So today the southern side of the causeway, with its path, is much higher than that of the northern edge, which has a short drop to the water-meadows.

The best way to explore the salt marsh on the south side of Exceat Bridge and the water-meadows to the north up to Litlington is to walk along either side of the river bank itself. The meadows and marshes can be visited by using the many gates for access to fields and wooden planks to cross ditches.

Early on a cold, clear, crisp, January day, as dawn was breaking and the ground was covered with frost, I walked over the Seven Sisters from Birling Gap, and I will never forget the quite astonishing sight that greeted me as I gazed down on the Meanders from the top of Haven Brow. Hundreds of different species of duck – *goldeneye, tufted, pochard* and *mallard* – sat motionless in the areas of water not frozen over. *Canada geese*, too, grazed amongst the frost-topped grasses along the water's edge, uttering occasional 'aa-honk' noises which reverberated in the still air. A *kestrel* sat frozen on a post beside the path and allowed me to close to almost a metre's distance before it lazily flew off into the cold, clear dawn.

On walking further into the valley and along the side of the Meanders, my eye was caught by a vivid green spot silhouetted against the brown earth of the water's bank. On closer inspection with binoculars, this turned out to be a *kingfisher* bent on catching a small fish from a patch of unfrozen water. The kingfisher is a bird which can be seen occasionally in the area of the Cuckmere. In springtime several birds can be seen at a time flying low and straight and very swiftly over the water, looking for shoals of small fish. Occasionally you will see one hover before plunging into the water after its prey. How it avoids hitting its head on the bottom when the water is shallow is a mystery. The birds, once seen, are seldom forgotten, with their brilliant azure blue-green upper parts, white throat and sharp-pointed bill. They nest further up the Cuckmere in holes bored in the river bank only a few centimetres above the water level. At the end of this hole, about one metre deep, between five and eight pure white eggs are laid on the bare earth in March or April. A few fish bones are added as nest material by the parent bird during incubation. In spring spates the nest is liable to be flooded, with the consequent loss of eggs and young. However, like many birds, the kingfisher will lay a second clutch later on in June or July, and this will have a better chance of success. A kingfisher's nesting hole can be distinguished from that of a rat or sand martin by its circular appearance. Piles of fresh earth below the hole indicates that the nest is recent, and later on droppings will indicate that it is in use. It is an interesting fact that birds that nest in holes almost invariably lay white eggs, possibly because the need for protective coloration is absent.

The *redshank* can often be heard on the lower Cuckmere marshes, with its repeated 'tew, tew, tew' call alerting all the other birds on the marsh when it is disturbed. As a boy I often found its nest of four eggs laid in a tuft of reeds, but sadly disturbance by humans and possibly over-grazing by cattle and sheep has led to its decline in the area, and I do not believe that it is likely to nest and successfully rear young here now.

The *lapwing* is another bird that is on the decline, and now only infrequently does it attempt to make a small scrape lined with grass on the ground as a nest on which to lay its four beautifully camouflaged eggs. Its decline is almost certainly due to a combination of disturbance and the predations of the fox, crow and wild mink, the latter being a comparatively recent pest which has spread from fur farms and become naturalised. How sad that no longer is it common to see the lapwing's acrobatic display flight and its repeated calling 'pee-wi, pee-wi' in the springtime over the lower Cuckmere. However, the *peewit* (as it is known still by country folk) is common on our northern pastures, and large flocks migrate south in autumn. It is these flocks which can often be seen feeding on invertebrates, seeds and vegetable matter in the valley in late September through to March. So we can still watch these handsome, richly coloured birds with their graceful, rhythmic flight even though we have almost lost the haunting, romantic quality of their voices heralding spring and the breeding cycle.

If there is just one bird to choose from which is characteristic of the area, it must be the *heron*. Haunting marshes, lakes and river, the heron is easily recognised by its large size, dark bluish-grey wings, black eye streak and powerful dagger-shaped bill. You can watch the birds, sometimes from quite close, standing motionless for long periods in or beside water. They seem oblivious to any outside distraction as they concentrate intensely on watching for their prey of frogs or small fish. Make a move, however, and they will be off, uttering a deep harsh 'frarnk' and flying powerfully with slow, deep wing-beats. This is one bird that has increased in numbers around the river, and it now nests in the tops of tall trees somewhere in the valley. It is one of the first birds to breed and returns year after year to the same colony, where it lays its two to four eggs in a nest of sticks, moss and hair in February and March. Let us hope that this lovely, graceful bird continues to increase and give pleasure to those from towns and cities who observe it closely for perhaps the first time.

Numerous other bird species can be seen, but space is not available to describe them all. Try making a list yourself with dates and time and compare it from year to year. You may be lucky and see one of the more uncommon birds, as I did when walking under High-and-Over on a July day when the river was low and the sun was high in the sky. Amongst the *sandpipers* and *black-headed gulls* feeding on uncovered and muddy banks, I spotted a small snow white heron-like bird with a black bill and yellow feet. A *little egret* to be sure, and in recent years this bird has been spotted more and more often along the marshes of the south coast. I wonder if global warming has had an effect here, as the bird was only an occasional visitor to our islands in the past. Who can tell whether soon it will nest among the bushes and trees of the valley?

One place not to be missed is the area of tall reeds and open water called Charleston Reed Bed. This is owned by Eastbourne College, and access is by a small path just south of the driveway to Charleston Manor. Both the *reed* and *sedge warblers* nest here, as does the *reed bunting* and *whitethroat*. During the spring and autumn use your binoculars in this exciting place and count the number of different warblers and other migrants that you can spot. The undergrowth and scrub in the area provides excellent cover for our commoner resident birds like *long-tailed tits, wrens* and even the *sparrowhawk*.

The river is tidal all the way upstream to Milton Lock, just north of Alfriston, and the effect of salt water makes an impact on the environment of this stretch of water. At low tide, when the river is very shallow and trickling only slowly over the rocks, walk along the river bank below White Bridge at Litlington in August or September. The sweet smell of seaweed lying dark green on the mud fills the air, and one's ear picks up the almost imperceptible 'plop, plop, plopping' noise in the water. Suddenly one sees it – a dark grey fin and then the grey body of a *mullet* perhaps four kilograms in weight, breaking water. Then, as one's eye becomes adjusted to the murky water and its deception of colour, depth and reflections, one sees not one fish but shoals of large mullet feeding on invertebrates in the mud. One can almost reach down and pluck them out, but to try is to risk getting stuck in the soft estuarine mud. The fish are wary, with a strong sense of sound and sight, and really one cannot get very close. Better to watch them from the safety of the bridge.

Autumn is fast approaching, and young *lapwings*, *sandpipers* and *ringed plovers* can be seen feeding beside the river. In the water-meadows a *shelduck*, distinctive with its black, white and chestnut plumage and bright red bill, forages around for grubs and insects. Flocks of *goldfinches*, with their bold head markings of scarlet, black and white, and black and yellow wings, chatter among the thistle heads on which they feed. High above, *swallows* gather as they have their last feed of insects before migrating south. Soon the first winter frosts carpet the valley in white, and on a quiet midwinter day only the *heron* patiently standing as a lone sentinel beside the water, and perhaps a scavenging *magpie*, remind one of the varied bird activity that only a few months ago dominated this beautiful place.

One of the first butterflies to be seen each year, as early as February, is the *brimstone*. This sulphur-coloured butterfly acquired its name because 'brimstone' is the old word for sulphur. It is a powerful flyer and roams for miles along hedgerows and thickets, especially in the area around High-and-Over. The butterfly itself feeds on the nectar of wild flowers, and its cater-pillar feeds on buckthorn. It often stays for long periods at one flower and always remains with its wings shut, probably because its underside blends in well with vegetation. This camouflage also helps it to hibernate successfully through the winter as a butterfly. It can still be seen in flight on warm autumn days as late as November, and can truly be said to be the first and last butterfly of the year.

In spring look out for a flash of metallic green of the *green hairstreak* below the scrub under High-and-Over. Unmistakeable, and, like the brimstone, it is seldom seen with its wings wide open. There are five different British hairstreak butterflies, and they get their name from the thin white line running across the underside of each wing, but in the case of the green hairstreak this is reduced to a row of white dots. The bright metallic green colour of the butterfly is produced by the effect of light on the tiny scales on the wings which act as prisms and only let in the green colour of the spectrum. Green hairstreaks are hardly ever seen feeding on flowers, as instead they seem to spend their time flying in short, swift bursts, chasing each other around bushes in secluded corners as they establish their territories.

Amongst a group of elm trees you may come across a plain brown butterfly, the *white-letter hairstreak*. This is an uncommon and local species which can be identified by the distinctive W mark traced out on its underside. It also has prominent black 'tails' tipped with white, at the rear of its wings. The white-letter hairstreak is on the wing in July and August and feeds on the nectar of bramble and privet flowers. The female lays her eggs singly on elm twigs, where they overwinter. The eggs hatch into small green caterpillars in the spring, which then feed on the newly formed buds, and later on the leaves and seeds. After the chrysalis stage the adult emerges in late June and lives for about 20 days.

On the downland slopes on either side of the river look out for the *common blue* butterfly, which is often seen flitting to and fro among the grass in June and July. As its name implies, this species of blue butterfly is widespread and quite common throughout Britain, and is at home on acid heathland as well as our chalk downlands. The reason for this is simple: the caterpillar feeds on several plants that are widespread too, such as clover and bird's-foot trefoil. The male is blue and the female is usually brown with orange markings around the wings. Just to confuse, sometimes the female can be found in a blue form but still with orange markings around the wings. Both sexes have white margins around the wing edges. The eggs are laid singly on the food plant, and the green caterpillars, after feeding, hibernate in winter. The chrysalis is formed in spring. This stage lasts for about two weeks. The adults emerge in April but are best seen in May, June and July. Two generations are produced each year, and the adult lives for only about two or three weeks. Often you will see groups of males clustered around puddles drinking the water for their mineral content. As the sun goes down in the evening you may also find a number of common blues clinging to grass stems, resting with their heads pointed down. A difficult butterfly to get close to when the sun is shining brightly, but when the sun is blotted out by cloud and in the evening when it is low with little heat, then the butterfly can be easily approached and even touched. It is clearly attracted to the warmth of one's hand, and can often be seduced to perch on one's finger.

Heat is important to butterflies, and they need the sun's warmth to circulate the blood in their veins, so enabling them to fly. Moths, too, require heat to fly, and as most fly at night they can often be seen vibrating their wings furiously and increasing their body temperature by muscular activity. The wing scales of moths are thicker than butterflies' as a rule, and they act as a kind of insulating fur to retain body heat.

Before turning to the flowers of the area, it is worth pausing to reflect on the butterfly with its short lifespan and fragile appearance as an insect that has evolved from the great dragonflies of the carboniferous era some 350 million years ago that had wingspans of 60 centimetres.

The valley about Exceat supports a large variety of plants, some quite rare and found in few other places in Britain. Chief amongst these is one of the 50 or so different orchid species in the British Isles, the *early spider orchid*. One of the early orchids to flower, colonies of the plant can be found in late April and early May in certain places on the short turf of the downland slopes. It is a small plant, only some 10 to 20 centimetres tall, and is easily overlooked before the flowers open, because it is yellow-green in colour and blends in with its surroundings. Looking like fat round spiders, the flowers are large in comparison with the plant itself, and are rich brown in colour with yellow-green and light brown sepals. Near the top of the flower head are two glistening nectar pouches which look like a pair of eyes. These are obviously to attract insects, but observation of the plants has shown that few insects visit, and the production of ripe seed capsules is low – in the region of 6 to 18 per cent. The plant is perennial, but in some years there are no flowers, and a year or so may pass before the colonies reappear in all their glory. The reason for this is largely unknown. In the late winter the three or four lower leaves form a rosette, and are grey-green in colour with well-marked veins. They can be found, often with the edges burnt brown by frost, in February and March, well before a stem starts to appear. Like many of our orchids, the early spider's root system consists mainly of two egg-shaped tubers which act as a food store. An interesting fact about orchids is that in many cases the seed must become infected with a root fungus, mycorrhiza, before it can germinate. Mycorrhiza exists in the roots of many trees and plants, but the dependence of orchids on this fungus for its existence goes some way to explain why orchids are generally uncommon plants. The early spider orchid is found near the sea, and this characteristic probably links up with its western distribution on the European mainland, where it is quite common on the chalk downs of France. Sadly, like many of our orchids, this species is becoming rarer, possibly because it is on the edge of its range here in England, and even small climatic changes could affect its distribution.

In late spring the flowers in the valley on both sides of Exceat Bridge really come into their own. Many types of buttercup grow in the water-meadows and chalk grasslands, but one that is easily overlooked is the *celery-leaved buttercup*, which likes to grow on bare mud and can be easily recognised by its glossy five-sided leaves with very small yellow flowers. Another of the ranunculus or buttercup family is the *lesser spearwort*, to be found in damp places a few miles up from Exceat under High-and-Over. As its name implies, its leaves are long and spear-shaped. It can be distinguished from its near relative, the *greater spearwort*, by its small flowers and leaves, which do not have the bluish sheen of its much larger cousin. The greater spearwort is only found occasionally in the Cuckmere Valley, but it can be seen growing in profusion a few miles away at Friston Pond. The greater spearwort grows with its 'feet' submerged, whereas this is seldom the case with the lesser spearwort. Both plants flower in June and July. Like most of the buttercups, the spearworts exude an acrid poisonous juice when crushed, and are avoided by cattle. The leaves of the lesser spearwort have a burning taste, hence the Latin name *flammula* – 'a little flame'. Interestingly, ranunculus is derived from the Latin *rana* or 'frog', in allusion to damp meadows and ponds where most of the species are to be found.

One of the glorious sights of late spring is the sheet of white flowers that cover stretches of the water-filled ditches that lie to the east of the Cuckmere near Litlington. This is another member of the buttercup family, the *water crowfoot*, that has found white a more congenial colour than yellow in its aquatic environment. You will see, however, that it retains some of its pedigree's appearance by having yellow at the centre of the four-petalled flower. Unlike most buttercups, this species does not produce acrid poisonous juices, possibly because its environment generally precludes it from being browsed by cattle.

There are two uncommon plants that grow a short distance from the river below the Golden Galleon at Exceat Bridge. The first is *wild clary*, growing in late spring and summer, which can be recognised at a distance by its separate and apparently leafless whorls of violet-blue flowers. The name 'clary' is an ancient one derived from 'clear-eye'. Another old English name for the plant was '*see-bright*'. Friars and physicians of the Middle Ages found that the seeds of clary rapidly absorbed water and became mucilaginous. If placed in the corner of an eye, the mucilage picked up any small dust particles that had blown in. Clary grows on dry grassland favouring the chalk. You may also find it beside the path just below High-and-Over.

The second plant, *milk thistle*, is so unmistakeable and large that little difficulty should be found in locating it on the path up to Chyngton Farm. A long time ago it was introduced to the gardens of Western Europe and Britain from the Mediterranean, where its roots, young leaves and flower heads were used as food. Milk thistle grows some two metres tall, and derives its name from the large, dark green leaves that are intricately veined in white. This curious feature distinguishes it from all our other thistles. The solitary flower heads emerging in June or July are rosy-purple and surrounded by long yellowish spines. I remember first seeing it on a bright summer day with small puffy white cumulus clouds scudding across the sea over the Haven. What a sight this thistle made, with its striking leaves and purple flowers highlighted against the blue, white and green of the sea, sky and fields.

As summer approaches, the water-meadows alongside the river gradually become drier, but leaving little lines of depressions which remain damp sometimes the year through. These depressions, which were small rivulets in the winter, are now covered by that common but beautiful plant, *silverweed*. Easily recognised by its long, creeping and rooting runners with silky leaves covered with silvery hairs, it gives a silvery-grey appearance to the depressions when viewed from above. The large solitary flowers are uniformly yellow in colour and give a pleasing contrast to the rest of the plant. The Latin name, *anserina*, refers to the fact that geese are very fond of it, and probably explains why it is commonly found around duck-ponds.

From June to September, along the river banks and in the salt marsh of the estuary, look out for the *greater* and *lesser sea spurrey* growing in the grass on top of the mud. The latter has pink flowers with the petals much shorter than the sepals, whereas the former has larger pale pink, almost white, flowers, where the petals are the same size as the sepals. Both have fleshy leaves which act as a store of water when their habitat dries out.

In the still waters of the ditches can be found that pretty aquatic plant, the *frogbit*. With its white and yellow petals, it could be confused with the more numerous water crowfoot described earlier, but frogbit has only three petals and commences its display in July and August, just as the crowfoot has passed. It floats upon the surface of the water and sends out long horizontal runners which produce bunches of roots which descend and penetrate deeply into the mud. The runners also produce groups of kidney-shaped leaves, which help to highlight the flowers that grow on stout stalks above them.

Flowering at the same time and in similar conditions to frogbit, the *water plantain* has very large leaves supported on long, thick but soft stalks. From the centre of the leaf bases the flowering stem rises up to one and a half metres, producing branches of lilac-white flowers at intervals up the stem. The thick fleshy base of the plant is rich in starch, and when its acrid nature is lost through drying, it can be used as a source of food. Certain Central Asian peoples, such as the Kalmucks of Mongolia, so use it, and the Chinese actually cultivate it.

Growing next to the water plantain in a few places, you may come across a beautiful plant which, once seen, will always be remembered: the *flowering rush*. This has a tall flower stem almost two metres high, on top of which are clusters of large rosy flowers three centimetres across. Before it flowers in July and August it is easily overlooked because its long slender sword-shaped leaves merge with other aquatic vegetation. Its Latin name, *butomus*, is derived from the Greek words *bous*, an ox, and *tomos*, cutting, implying that oxen are sometimes cut by the leaves of the plant when they are drinking.

Another plant of the muddy edges of the water-filled ditches is one of the many species of forget-me-not, the *water forget-me-not*. This plant often forms in large colonies, and the area is lit up with its beautiful pale blue flowers. Our forefathers knew this plant as the *water mouse-ear scorpion-grass*, because as the buds open in succession, so the stalk lengthens and curves in the shape of a scorpion's tail. The Latin name of the species, *myosotis*, derives from two Greek words meaning 'mouse-ear', which refers to the hairiness and shape of the leaves. In the Middle Ages the stem of this plant was worn as a symbol of love by young people, and its original name was slowly replaced by the present-day 'forget-me-not'.

On the chalk slopes of High-and-Over can be found the rare *white horehound*. It grows in clumps up to a metre tall, with typical 'mint-shaped' leaves, which in this species are green above and white beneath. The plant is densely covered with cottony hairs, giving it a hoary appearance. The flowers, unlike most of the mint family to which it belongs, are white in colour. Its present rarity could be due to the fact that it is a valued herb used as a cure for coughs. Lozenges containing an extract from its leaves are still sold in shops today.

26

While on the slopes of High-and-Over, look out for the small *basil thyme*, which is highly aromatic. Another plant of the mint family, this was used in the Middle Ages as a cure for diseases of the heart and as an antidepressant. Look closely at its lilac-coloured flowers and note the white mark on the lower lip which guides bees to its nectar. A characteristic of the plant is that its stem, about 18 centimetres long, lies along the ground for half its length before rising into the air. Another similar plant growing nearby, but which does not show this characteristic, is *calamint*. Again, this is an aromatic herb, this time used for making a herbal tea. Both plants flower at the same time, in July and August.

Look out for the *star thistle* growing in a number of places on the hillsides and beside the pathways. It is easily recognised by the yellow spines surrounding the rose-purple flower heads that bloom from July to September. The whole plant is about 60 centimetres tall, with a stiff and much branched stem. The star thistle is a rare plant which seems to be holding its own and perhaps increasing in this area, one of its strongholds in Sussex. It is said that the sharp spines with the seed heads get caught in the hooves of cattle, and this enables it to spread itself around the area. Its Latin name, *calcitrapa*, refers to the metal spikes which in Roman times were strewn across roads to injure the hooves of advancing enemy horses. These spikes always ended up with at least one spike pointing upwards, similar to the spines of the star thistle.

One of my favourite flowers of late summer is the *marsh mallow*, found growing on the inside of the river bank just beside the bridge at Litlington. It is easily recognised by its large size (1.5 metres tall) and its velvety, downy leaves and stem. The large pale-pink flowers contrast pleasingly with the overall grey appearance of the plant. Once quite common on salt marshes in southern England and Wales, it is now becoming rarer as these habitats are drained. In years past it was dug up in quantities from the marshes around London, and marshmallow confectionery was made from its dried and powdered roots. Today's marshmallows are made of sugar and gelatine!

See if you can find an unusual clover, the *strawberry-headed clover*, which grows on the grassy banks of the river below Litlington, sometimes in the form of a grassy cushion. It is easily recognised when the pink flowers are over in late summer and autumn, and the seed heads swell and take on the appearance and colour of strawberries.

The last plant to be considered in this chapter is the *sea aster*, which is common along the river bank, where it thrives in the salt-water environment. Nearly a metre tall, with fleshy leaves, it produces star-shaped mauve flowers from late July to October. An unusual variety of this plant, without the mauve petals, can also be found growing alongside the normal variety in this stretch of tidal river.

Frogs and *toads* are an important species in the lower Cuckmere, and visitors to the area are reminded of their presence in February each year, when signs are erected along the roadside to warn motorists of their migratory habits. For these amphibians, which in the winter have hibernated under the bushes and trees to the east of the valley, wake up and make their way by day and night to the water-meadows and ditches near the river. It is at this time that the males find their voices, their throats swell and the valley comes alive with their croaking. Females respond with chirps and grunts, and their thousands of eggs are laid in the water; frogs' eggs in the form of spawn and toads' eggs in a jelly-like string. Frogs' eggs hatch at the end of May into tadpoles, and by mid-July they have changed into tiny two-centimetre miniature adults. They then jump out of the water and up the banks of ditches and disappear into the countryside, feeding on small insects, slugs, snails and earthworms. Within three years they are fully grown adults able to mate and reproduce. These creatures form an important part of the food supply, as the eggs, tadpoles and adults are preyed upon by fish, newts, water birds, snakes, rats, and hedgehogs. Only their phenomenal reproduction rate ensures the species survive.

You will come across many beautiful and sometimes rare insects in the course of your exploration of the meadows and marshes. Look out for the many kinds of dragonfly that abound in the area, such as the *hairy dragonfly* and the bright red *ruddy darter dragonfly*.

Beetles of all kinds are to be found, especially ladybirds. There are 44 species of ladybird in the country, the commonest being the *seven-spot ladybird*. But see if you can find the species with 19 spots, a characteristic wetland insect. Ladybirds have a voracious appetite for aphids of all kinds and are therefore the friend of the farmer and gardener alike. Adult ladybirds hibernate throughout the winter in crevices or under the bark of trees. They emerge in spring and fly off to aphid-infested plants and lay their eggs. The eggs hatch in about a week into long-legged grubs which feed on the aphids. After about four weeks the grub turns into a chrysalis, which attaches itself to a leaf. This in turn hatches out into a ladybird beetle about a week later. The striking colours of the ladybird species, black, yellow and red, are a warning to predatory birds that they are poisonous. Indeed, when attacked they exude a nasty-tasting fluid containing alkaloid poisons.

This chapter would not be complete without a word on some important trees that grow in the area. The tallest and most striking *white willow* in Sussex can be found along the western side of the Litlington road about 800 metres to the north of Charleston Manor. The underside of its leaves are covered with white silky hairs, and when the slender branches are swaying to and fro in a summer breeze they give the willow a lightness of colour unique amongst British trees. Look out for it, pause and ponder upon its beauty.

Some of the most attractive *English elms* in the county grow in the grounds of Charleston Manor, and can be seen when the Manor is open to the public. The English elm, before the outbreak of Dutch elm disease in the 1970s, was a common sight along our hedgerows, where they were planted deliberately by eighteenth-century landowners. When tenant farmers began to enclose the old open fields with hawthorn hedges, the landowners required them to plant elms at intervals for shade, shelter and timber. These elms were raised from nursery stock, and when the mature trees were felled they were replaced automatically by the sucker shoots that spring vigorously from their roots. Dutch elm disease is caused by a beetle burrowing into the tree and spreading a fungus that destroys the wood tissue just below the bark. Many of the elms in southern England and South Wales have died as a result of the disease, and great efforts are now being made to eradicate and prevent its spread. Sadly, our landscape characterised by tall, elegant English elms has changed dramatically with their loss.

Heron

4

WEST DEAN AND FRISTON FOREST

To 'discover' West Dean and explore Friston Forest, take the small road that leads east off the Exceat to the Litlington road. After a kilometre or so you will arrive at the picturesque backwater of West Dean, which has links of much historical interest.

King Alfred the Great had a house in West Dean in the ninth century, of which there is nothing left now, but signs of the existence of a large manor farm are all around: flint barns, stables and other outbuildings. That troubled great Saxon King chose his site well, as West Dean was protected by hills and hidden by trees, as well as being secluded and remote. At that time the Cuckmere Haven was a larger and deeper inlet than now, and the sea probably came up to the very edge of the village itself. Who knows, but possibly a jetty existed where the duck-pond is now. Certainly the King would not have chosen a place that did not have easy access to the sea, which for Sussex, with its hinterland of clay and forest, was almost the only means of travel. We know a little of this era from the writings of Bishop Asser, who was chaplain and later biographer to the King. He wrote about events of that time and told how he was summoned from various parts of Britain to meet the King at West Dean.

West Dean also has one of the oldest inhabited rectories in the country. This building, situated just below the church, dates from about AD 1280 and is built of stone and flint with a spiral stone staircase, huge oak beams and lancet windows deeply splayed on the inside.

West Dean is dominated by Friston Forest, which surrounds it. One way to appreciate its beauty is to stand on the top of High-and-Over and look across the river towards the forest on a clear spring day before the first leaves on the trees have opened. You will see a purplish hue which is caused by the light reflected off the buds of millions of the beech trees that predominate in the Forest.

Planting of the Forest was started in 1926 by the Forestry Commission, the intention being to establish a beech forest with conifers as protection. However, as the latter grow faster than the harder beechwood, for a long time only conifers could be seen, and the Commission received much criticism for covering the Downs with such an uninteresting and monotonous landscape. The conifers are now being cut at the rate of about ten acres per year and sold for pulp, and the beech is really coming into its own. By the end of this century Friston Forest will be almost pure beech, with here and there little patches of pine and sycamore. By the middle of the next century the Forest is expected to be the finest beech woodland in the country, covering some 1,500 acres and containing over 4 million trees.

The area of Friston Forest is now owned by South East Water, who lease it to the Forestry Commission. South East Water have an active management system to ensure that the natural environment is protected and encouraged to flourish for the quiet enjoyment of the public.

What a habitat for birds! You are likely to see just about anything in and around the Forest. Most years in spring *red kites* are seen resting in the rides on their way from the Continent to Wales and central England, where they breed. The *osprey* too is seen quite often in early spring, perched on tree stumps and tearing away at freshly caught fish from the Cuckmere River or Arlington Reservoir. A *golden oriole*, with its unmistakeable brilliant yellow body and black wings and tail, was spotted perched on a beech branch one cold January day a few years ago. The beautifully plumaged *hoopoe*, a rare spring visitor, very occasionally makes itself known in forest clearings by its far-carrying cry 'poo-poo-poo', which echoes through the woods.

Two of the three British resident woodpeckers nest in the Forest. Woodpeckers make their nest by pecking a hole into any tree which has a rotten centre. The nest is usually just a bare scrape or a few woodchips at the bottom of a 60-centimetre shaft down the excavated centre. On this the hen bird lays her four to seven white eggs in April or May. The same nest can be used year after year, but often the bird drills another nest just below the first; so after a few years a line of holes, one upon another, appear on the tree – a sure sign of nesting woodpeckers.

The presence of woodpeckers is most often indicated by their characteristic tattoo of regular knocking, which resonates through the still Forest. This noise, frequently heard when nest-building is taking place, is also used as a territorial 'song' to warn other woodpeckers to keep out of their area.

The woodpecker you will most often see is the *green woodpecker*, which walks over the grassy rides in search of ants and their nests. It uses its long worm-like tongue to lick up and devour the ants, their pupae and larvae. The green woodpecker is easily recognised, for, as its name suggests, it has dark green upper parts with paler underparts and a crimson crown. Its loud laughing call, which echoes through the woodland glades, gives the bird its country name '*yaffle*'. Its call and deep undulating flight pattern make it unmistakeable.

The *greater spotted woodpecker* is fairly widespread throughout the forest, and, because it is fond of nuts, is often seen at garden bird tables in nearby villages. Unfortunately, it also has a fondness for nestlings, and raids other birds' nests for food. It has also learnt to break open nest boxes. The greater spotted woodpecker can be recognised by its distinct black and white plumage; the male (but not the female) has a crimson nape patch. Both sexes have a red patch under the tail.

The *lesser spotted woodpecker*, the third of our resident species, is much rarer, and to my knowledge has not been seen, probably because of its liking for older trees that are rotting and fallen down, not a characteristic of this relatively young forest.

All of our common garden birds are represented in the Forest: the *blackbird, chaffinch, blue tit, robin, wren* and *hedge sparrow*. The *song thrush* too is fairly common in the Forest, but sadly it is on the decline as a bird of the garden, possibly because the snails on which it feeds are often contaminated by the use of modern slug pellets. Look out for large flint rocks surrounded by broken snail shells, for this will indicate the song thrush's 'anvil' on which it breaks open the snails. It augments its diet with berries and insects, and makes its nest in an enormous range of sites, but in early spring it usually nests about two metres up in a deciduous bush or hedge where it is well hidden. The nest of grasses and mud is lined with mud, unlike that of the blackbird, which is similar but lined with grass. The song thrush's three to six eggs are light blue with black spots and are laid as early as February, with repeat clutches on to August. The song thrush has a beautiful song, sung in most months of the year from a song perch, where the bird sits, often with its head cocked to one side. The song is loud and musical, with short, varied phrases repeated two to four times.

The *mistle thrush*, a larger version of the song thrush, but with a much harsher and less musical song, can be seen usually on the forest edges within easy reach of fields and meadows. Feeding mainly on berries, it gets its name from the fact that it is one of the few birds that feeds on those of mistletoe. The mistle thrush also likes worms, grubs and insects, and can often be seen in small groups in winter 'grazing' for these in the fields around the Forest. The nest is a substantial structure of grasses and other vegetation and is built more than three metres up in the fork of a tree. The three to six pale blue eggs, with blotches of reddish-brown, are laid as early as March, with repeat clutches until late June. Be careful when near its nest of young, because I have known an irate parent bird to dive down and attack with a loud scolding noise – quite alarming, and certainly a deterrent to other birds or animals. On cold January or February days the mistle thrush is almost the only bird that sings, and even in a storm it can be seen at the top of a leafless tree throwing its notes out on a desolate countryside. No wonder this bird has another, less common, name: '*the stormcock*'.

A bird of prey that frequents the forest is the *sparrowhawk*, which because of its shy and secretive habit is not as well known as the kestrel seen hovering along our roads and motorways. Incidentally, of our birds of prey, only the kestrel and buzzard hover. If you see a grey-brown shape flitting low along a forest ride or along a hedgerow early in the morning or late in the evening, then it is likely to be a sparrowhawk. During the breeding season the birds remain very unobtrusive. The nest is built high up in the top of trees close to the main trunk and consists of a platform of twigs. The five white eggs, blotched with pale and dark rich brown markings, are laid from April to June. The young hatch in about 35 days, and as they grow in size they become very noisy. This is the time when the nest and birds are more easily located. I once had the good fortune of seeing a male sparrowhawk at close quarters just beneath my bedroom window on a garden post. It was a freezing cold February morning, and the bird with its closely barred red-brown underparts and yellow legs was intent on swooping on any bird or small animal that dared show itself. After an hour or so it got bored or cold and just flew off without any obvious signs of success.

At one time, when Britain was heavily wooded, the sparrow-hawk was certainly one of our most abundant birds of prey, but as the woodland was felled in the nineteenth century so their population decreased. This clever and cunning bird, however, survived in large numbers in the remoter undisturbed woods and forests, and even persecution from gamekeepers protecting their masters' stocks did not seriously deplete their numbers. However, the advent and widespread use of pesticides on the land in the 1950s and 1960s decimated their population. This was especially so in East Anglia, where seed-feeding birds, the hawk's main prey, were affected by toxic seed dressings. DDT too had its effect on the environment, as, unlike other poisons, its derivatives are extremely stable. It is this stability that makes it such a danger to wildlife, because its toxicity stores up and remains in the body of its victim, be it insect or plant. In the case of the sparrowhawk, DDT was the cause of a large fall-off in breeding success, measured by the number of young reared per egg. Since 1964 there has been more control of the use of toxic substances by farmers, and the sparrowhawk population has increased in most areas. It is certainly increasing now in Friston Forest.

Many warblers breed in the Forest, and it is difficult to choose one that is more dominant than another. Perhaps the *blackcap* is one of my favourites. A migrant, it arrives in early April after a flight of nearly 6,000 kilometres from tropical Africa, and adver-tises its presence by its rich warbling song. Easily recognised by its overall grey colour, the male has a glossy black crown, and the female a red-brown crown. Like that other songster of the forest, the *garden warbler*, the blackcap builds its nest of grass, roots and straw, lined with fine hair, in brambles and thickets about one to three metres off the ground. It is well hidden, and because of its flimsy construction it is often strengthened with wool or spiders' webs. Both warblers lay between four and six similar greenish-white eggs, blotched and spotted with various shades of deep olive, in May and June. Both these warblers seem to prefer the areas of blackthorn thickets in the Forest.

Three pairs of *long-eared owl* nest in the Forest, using the old nests of magpies or crows. This nocturnal bird is difficult to observe, for it roosts by day in thick foliage. However, I did see it once on a cold grey December day roosting in the grass on top of the Seven Sisters. You may be lucky enough to see one with its mottled buff and grey-brown plumage and long ear-tufts in the area of Charleston Bottom or Friston Pumping Station.

The *hobby* is a bird that is seen every summer in July to August, usually resting in trees beside the forest rides. This bird, looking like a small peregrine falcon, has a dashing flight and preys on small birds or flying insects, particularly at dusk. Its presence every summer suggests that it could be nesting nearby, although no young birds have been seen. It generally occupies the old nest of a carrion crow high up in a tree, and often it waits for the crow's young to vacate the nest before laying its two to four eggs in mid-June. You will know if you are close to a hobby's nest because if the bird flies off it will be very noisy, uttering a repeated 'pee-pee-pee' or 'wer-wer-wee-wee'. When the young are hatched, watch the male bringing food back to the nest. Look out for this uncommon bird of prey when in the Forest – hopefully you may be the first to confirm it nesting here.

With its rich variety of vegetation, verdant clearings and wide paths rich in plant life, the Forest supports a good variety of butterflies. The *speckled wood* is perhaps one of the most familiar to be found inhabiting the woodland margins in early spring. Its brown and buff speckled wings give it camouflage in the dappled sunlight that percolates the leaf canopy of its habitat. The male, which has smaller buff spots than the female, settles in patches of sunlight where a female is more likely to see and be attracted to it. This butterfly shows a high degree of territorial behaviour, and the male will defend its patch of woodland by attacking any intruder in a series of up and down flights. As with most butterflies, scent produced from the base of the wing scales plays an important part in the speckled wood's short lifespan of only 20 days. The male almost certainly marks its territory by scent, which is also a possible attraction to the female. The eggs are laid twice a year any time from spring to autumn on the leaves of various grasses. The green caterpillars emerge in 10 days and then feed at night on grasses for about 30 days. They then turn into chrysalids before the new butterfly emerges some 30 days later. Autumn caterpillars live throughout the winter, actively feeding only on warm days, and take some eight or nine months to become fully grown.

On the road near Friston Pumping Station, look out for the largest of our nine fritillary butterflies, the *silver-washed fritillary.*

The orange-red spotted wings have a span of some seven centimetres, and the butterflies can be seen feeding off bramble flowers and thistles from July to September. This butterfly is a true woodland species, and is unique in Britain in laying its eggs on tree trunks and not on a food plant. The spiny caterpillars hatch out in two weeks, eat their eggshells, hibernate in the winter and then descend to feed on the leaves of the violet plant.

Fluttering around bushes and trees in March and as late as October is the *holly blue*. The female is easily distinguished from other members of the blue family by having black wing-tips on its upper sides. The undersides of both sexes are a delicate pale blue quite unlike any other. The holly blue favours holly trees in spring and ivy-covered trees and walls in the summer – look for it in such habitats in the Forest.

The *white admiral*, with its distinctive black wings with a white band running across them, is relatively new to the Forest, and is still an uncommon sight. Search for it on the northern edges near Lullington Heath. The best time to see it is on a sunny day in July, when the males, in marking their territory, swoop low over the woodland before soaring high up into the trees to rest. They can also be seen feeding on bramble flowers, their favourite source of nectar. The female seeks out *honeysuckle*, the sole food plant of the caterpillar, on which to lay its eggs in July. The egg hatches after about a week, and the caterpillar feeds until the autumn, when it spins silken threads to attach itself to the honeysuckle leaf. It hibernates throughout the winter within the, by now, crinkled leaf, emerging in spring to feed on the new green foliage. The chrysalid stage lasts about 12 days before the butterfly finally emerges in June. The adult lives for only about 25 days. The requirement for honeysuckle holds the key to this butterfly's existence in the Forest. Honeysuckle likes to grow rampant amongst unkempt hedges and shrubs, and it does not like to be 'managed'. This important factor, necessary for the continuing success of the white admiral, is being taken into account by the Forestry Commission and South East Water when essential management of the Forest is undertaken.

Friston Forest supports a wide variety of plant life, and there is only space to mention but a few of the more interesting or typical ones. Two plants that are common and found on the sides of the rides and byways are *hemp agrimony* and *ploughman's spikenard*. What chains of thought develop through one's mind as one contemplates the words that make up these names!

Hemp agrimony gets its name from the fact that its leaf shape suggests the foliage of the hemp plant used in India for the manufacture of rope and from which the drug cannabis is obtained. Flowering in July to October, this plant prefers the damper places in depressions and beside rivulets, anywhere where the soil is damp. However, surprisingly it is also found along the drier pathways and rides. Here it grows up to a metre tall and stands out well with its great masses of dull purple flower heads. The flowers contain honey and are a favourite refreshment place for butterflies such as the *red admiral*, *peacock* and *painted lady*.

Spikenard is a very ancient name mentioned in the Bible, and refers to a plant from India which has fragrant roots and medicinal properties in the form of perfumed ointment. This was costly to import, so poor people such as ploughmen had to be content with a less costly substitute which they found in plenty growing on the chalk soils of southern Britain. So the name ploughman's spikenard was given to this plant, which, when its leaves and roots are crushed, gives out a sweet-smelling fragrance. In July to September you will find this yellow-flowered, somewhat lacklustre, plant growing up to a metre tall on the banks of the many pathways and tracks in the Forest.

The reader will probably be surprised to find that two of our commoner woodland species, the *bluebell* and *wood anemone*, are almost absent from the Forest, but what it lacks in quantity it makes up for in quality. The rare *pheasant's eye*, that beautiful bright crimson-red flower, appears any time between May and September. It prefers disturbed ground, and can be found around some of the newer car parks. The chalk inclines beside some of the wider tracks in the Forest are another favourite place for this flower, and forest management now includes the raking of this habitat to encourage its growth. The pheasant's eye is a native of Continental Europe, western Asia and North Africa, and has been introduced into this country. Its Latin name, *adonis*, is very ancient and perpetuates the myth that the blood of Adonis fell upon this flower when he was killed by the wild boar.

Another rare plant of the wayside tracks and growing amongst the taller grass is the *yellow vetchling*. The pale yellow flowers are borne singly on long stalks and emerge in May and June. The plant is easily recognised by having enlarged spear-shaped stipules (not leaves) which clasp the stem. The small leaflets apparent in the young plants finish off as tendrils, enabling it to climb up the grasses that surround it. The stem is up to eight centimetres long. Not to be confused with yellow vetchling is *yellow vetch*, which grows in similar habitats in the Forest. The solitary pale yellow flowers blooming in June to August have very short stalks and the leaves have from five to seven pairs of narrow oval leaflets. See if you can find either or both of these plants in the south-western part of Friston Forest.

The grass verges of the main road just to the south side of the Forest are a haven for wild flowers. In places the plants have been protected from roadside cutting by green conservation posts erected by the District Council. These posts are a relatively new idea and are designed to conserve particularly uncommon species which have been reported to the council by members of the public or conservation groups. Two particular species that are to be found between the posts in this area are *sainfoin* and *chicory*.

Grown as a fodder plant in some places, sainfoin is considered to be native to our chalk Downs and not just an escape from cultivation. It is a handsome herb up to half a metre tall, with pea-like flower which are pink with dark veins running through them. It flowers in June to August and is easily seen on the roadside. Sainfoin comes from the French word meaning wholesome hay or fodder.

The chicory plant was once a familiar and common plant of the dry roadside, especially on the chalk, but sadly it is now a fairly rare sight. Up to a metre tall and flowering in June to October, this plant has large dandelion-shaped flowers, five centimetres in diameter, bright pale blue in colour, quite unlike any other wild British plant. The fleshy root stock, when roasted and ground up, is used for making coffee which is popular on the Continent. For this reason it is cultivated on a large scale in Belgium and Guernsey. Look out for this strikingly beautiful plant amongst the roadside grasses.

Of the orchid species, three are of particular note. The *white helleborine*, flowering in May and June, can be found amongst the beech trees in the eastern central part of the Forest. Although not a tall plant, being only some 15 to 40 centimetres in height, here in Friston Forest they grow over 60 centimetres tall and are very conspicuous, with their creamy-white flowers and fresh green leaves standing out well against the bare carpet of rich-brown dead beech litter. The taller plants are found growing near the woodland edge where there is more light. The fibrous roots penetrate deeply into the dead leaves and soil to as much as 40 centimetres. The flowers are frequented by wasps, which have no tongue, and therefore the nectar is held easily accessible in a hollow in the case of the lip. The seed may take eight years to set and a further three years may elapse before flowers appear. Thus you may find in any large colony of these helleborines a number of non-flowering immature plants.

The *broad-leaved helleborine* is another orchid of note, and its imposing flower spike of up to a hundred pink and brown flowers can be found almost anywhere in July to September. Up to some 90 centimetres tall, its flowers are again frequented almost entirely by wasps. Why this is so is not really known, as the copious nectar is easily accessible to other insects. It is quite a sight to see this orchid spike absolutely covered in wasps in late August and September. They do their work well, as one can see from the numbers of flowers that have had their pollinia removed. Like other helleborines, the seeds take at least eight years to develop into flowering plants.

Occasionally, and in only one or two of the darkest parts of the Forest, can be seen the *bird's-nest orchid*. A true saprophyte, this orchid relies on mycorrhizal infection of its roots, which feeds it with nutriment by breaking down the rotted beech leaves through which it grows. The plant, some 20 to 50 centimetres high, is all of the same colour, a warm yellowish-brown. Where there should be leaves are long brown scales which clasp the stem. The flowers appear in May and June, and contain nectar and large masses of bright yellow pollen, which have a pleasant smell of honey that attracts many sorts of small flies and thrips.

Not to be confused with an orchid of the same name is the *yellow bird's-nest*. This saprophytic plant, again relying on benevolent mycorrhiza fungus for its nutrition, puts out its yellow fleshy stem some 20 centimetres high from amongst the beech leaves in June. The drooping dingy yellow fragrant flowers appear in July, and, after fertilisation, they stand out horizontally with only the uppermost ones becoming erect. Friston Forest has probably the greatest concentration of this plant in the British Isles. Look for it in the darker areas of beech wood just north of the track from the Pumping Station to West Dean.

The last plant of note in this chapter is a rare dock, the *golden dock*, which was very common once around the duck-pond at West Dean. Due to recent clearance of the vegetation around the edge of the pond in recent years, this distinctive plant, 40 centimetres tall, is now largely confined to the island in the middle. The golden dock, its name derived from the golden colour it turns into when in fruit, requires a wet, muddy habitat rich in both nitrogen and phosphorous. This species has declined sharply in Britain due to the drainage of wetlands, but its robust nature should enable it to survive, given suitable conditions. The use of ponds by cattle and waterfowl where it already exists should give it the nutrients necessary for it to flourish.

Within the Forest are a number of dew-ponds which existed on the downland many years before the Forest was planted. The origins and age of dew-ponds are surrounded in controversy and mystery. Some people say they were constructed in the Saxon period, but more likely they were started in about the seventeenth century. What we do know is that they were carefully constructed of straw, clay and flints, and were positioned to catch the mist that sweeps over the Downs from the sea throughout the year. It is mist and not dew that maintains the water level in the ponds, so that even in the harshest drought the ponds seldom dry out. Dew provides only an insignificant amount of water, perhaps only five centimetres a year, and rain falling directly some 90 centimetres. Both would not be sufficient in themselves to maintain water levels for the many animals and livestock that use them. Modern dew-ponds constructed before the Second World War are made with a concrete lining, but these do have a tendency to crack in the frosts of winter.

The dew-ponds scattered throughout the Forest are the home of one of our uncommon amphibians, the *great crested newt*. The largest of all the European species, this newt can be recognised by its size, up to 18 centimetres long, and in the case of the male by its high denticulated crest in springtime. All the newts have some ability to change colour to suit their surroundings, and their skin is periodically shed during life. In the case of the great crested newt the skin is covered with warty glands which give off a fluid which is distasteful to would-be predators. Mating starts in March, and the female lays her 200 to 300 jelly-like eggs from early April to early July. After about nine weeks these have developed into small but recognisable newts, and after five months the metamorphosis is complete. Adult newts leave the pond in August, and in late October and November they creep into holes or crevices to hibernate through the winter, only to reappear in March when the temperature begins to warm up. Great crested newts are long-lived creatures, and have been known to live for up to 27 years. This lovely creature is a bonus for the Forest, and its existence must be protected for future generations to admire and enjoy.

The Forest is home to many types of fungi. When the first autumn rains begin and the leaf litter becomes damp and there is an aroma of decay, then fungal mycelium begin their work. In the

41

woods just to the north-west of Friston Pumping Station you can find up to 50 or so different species of fungi on a typical rainy day in October, with such exotic names as *dead man's fingers, wood woolly-foot, deceiver, rooting shank* and *plums and custard.* Space allows only a few to be described in this chapter.

The *puffball* is commonly seen in open fields and lawns, but here in the Forest a slightly different variety grows, with a layer of pyramidal warts on the white upper head and a distinct stem some three to four centimetres long. When young and the flesh is white, the puffball can be cut up, fried and eaten. The *wood mushroom* can be found growing nearby, a much bigger fungi than the puffball, with a white cap some five to twelve centimetres across, and white, then pinkish and finally sepia brown, gills underneath. The flesh when broken smells of anise. On the path up from the Pumping Station to Friston Pond look out for the *earth star* fungus, which grows amongst the leaf litter. Aptly named, this fungus is most often seen after the onion-shaped brown fruit body has split radially into a star-like pattern six to ten centimetres across. The five flesh-like rays are light brown in colour, darkening with age. There are many other fungi growing in other parts of the Forest – be sure to identify them correctly from a good guidebook before attempting to try them out gastronomically.

Friston Forest has many moods, from the dark, sombre periods in winter to the bright and cheerful days of spring and summer. One can walk for miles along its tracks in winter without seeing people or being disturbed by noise, and even on the bleakest of days you can find shelter from the wind in hollows made deeper by the tall tees around, and from rain under coniferous branches.

Try taking a picnic in the Forest on a warm spring day when the sun's rays, still relatively low over the Downs, percolate through the first leaves on the trees. Sit on the green grass of one of the many south-facing rides and listen to the birds singing their hearts out from the branches. The peace and silence will enable you to contemplate the pressures and problems of this world and put them into perspective in comparison with the wonder and eternal grandeur of nature. You will be rejuvenated when you leave the Forest, and you will again have confidence to face the toil of day-to-day life.

Late autumn, too, can be a relaxing time to walk along the many byways, now with a covering of orange or brown leaves from the near-naked beeches. If the sun is shining, you can never get lost – remember if you point the hour hand of your watch towards the sun and draw a line between the hour hand and 12 o'clock, then this line will approximate to the north/south axis. It is more difficult to navigate if the sun is concealed by thick cloud, but moss and lichens do grow on the northern side of older forest trees, especially in winter.

Holiday times in the spring and summer bring an influx of people and mountain bikes and some of the seclusion and tranquillity is lost. But the Forest is large, and you can still find places, especially in the northern section, where you can be alone to watch birds and butterflies without disturbance. Solitude, peace and quietness is all too rare in this modern world of ours. What a pity if these very qualities special to the Forest are lost because of a lack of control on the number of visitors to it. A conflict of interests indeed for those responsible for the Forest's management.

I look forward to the next century, when Friston will become the finest beech forest in our country. Who knows, maybe those very rare orchids, the *red helleborine* and the *sword-leaved helleborine*, may return to grow in the county again amongst the beech leaves of the Forest floor.

Green Woodpecker

Stone Curlew

Plate 1   Cuckmere Haven, Page 9   Painting by Frank Wootton, OBE

Plate 2   Seven Sisters at Cuckmere Haven, Page 9   Painting by Frank Wootton, OBE

Plate 3   Stonechat, Page 11   M. Hollings

Plate 4   Clustered Bellflower, Page 16   H. M. Proctor

Plate 5   Common Rock Rose, Page 93   Author

Plate 6   Common Blue perched on finger, Page 22   Author

Plate 7   Kingfisher, Page 18   M. Hollings

Plate 8   Common Blues resting, Page 22   Author   Plate 9   Early Spider Orchid, Page 23   Author

Plate 10   Common Blues mating, Page 22   Author

Plate 11   Milk Thistle, Page 25   Author

Plate 12   Flowering Rush, Page 26   Author

Plate 13   White Horehound, Page 26   Author

Plate 14   Heron under High-and-Over, Page 19   Painting by Frank Wootton, OBE

Plate 15   Star Thistle, Page 27   Author

Plate 16   Sparrowhawk feeding young, Page 34   M. Hollings

Plate 17   Speckled Wood, Page 36   Author

Plate 18   Painted Lady, Page 12   Author

5

LULLINGTON HEATH

Lullington Heath lies just to the north of Friston Forest, and access is easiest by the path from Jevington Church or from Lullington Court. The Heath is an area of outstanding beauty and natural history, and was established as a National Nature Reserve as long ago as 1955.

If you choose to take the track up from Lullington Court, you will notice that it is sunken in places, which is an indication that it has an ancient origin. The heavy rainfalls early in 1995 uncovered a fascinating sight: on part of the path lower down near the road, the top layer of soil and rubble was washed away, revealing a layer of flintstones. These clearly formed the paving of the track many years ago when it was probably used for horse-drawn wagons. The flints are so well shaped and dressed that they probably came from the walls of Lullington Church, less than a kilometre away, after it was substantially destroyed many centuries ago. There is certainly no sign of the original church wall material to be found now, and one can only surmise that the flints were used to improve the local trackway leading to Jevington. What an interesting thought!

Ever since the early settlers moved off the Downs to cultivate the richer valley soils about 1,500 years ago, the Downs were left as pasture for grazing animals, mainly sheep. This was true of Lullington Heath, and it developed into a plant-rich grassland and chalk heath. Sheep-grazing continued until the Second World War, but was then stopped because the landowner, a water company, was concerned about the effects of animal pollution on the water supply. Lullington Heath and its neighbouring valley,

Deep Dene, together with Friston Forest, are all catchment areas for the Friston reservoir. The vegetation was kept under control by rabbits until their virtual elimination by myxomatosis in 1954. Coarse grasses then smothered the herbs and wild flowers, and hawthorn, gorse and wayfaring trees became rampant, leading to an invasion of scrubland typical of downland when grazing is not maintained. I can remember roaming the area as a boy in the early 1950s, when it was a wild place with large masses of close-cropped chalk heath with a few scattered low bushes and patches of bare chalk and flint.

Grazing restrictions were removed in the 1970s, but by that time scrub invasion had occurred in all areas of the reserve. The present owner, South East Water, leases the area to English Nature through the Forestry Commission. English Nature actively manage and maintain the area as a National Nature Reserve. Over the years rides have been cut through the scrub and a mowing programme has re-established the chalk heath flora. Sheep, goats and New Forest ponies have been introduced to browse scrub and thus produce a more diverse type of turf than that produced by mowing. Rabbits have now recovered strongly from myxomatosis and help greatly to control scrub encroachment. So active management has now produced open areas and has enabled the traditional short downland turf to reappear with its accompaniment of a rich flora and many insects, including rare butterflies. Many wild animals now inhabit and breed on the Reserve, such as *dormice*, *weasels*, *stoats*, *foxes* and *badgers*.

One May morning in 1951, when the mists were swirling over the Heath, I disturbed a *stone curlew*, which flew off low just ahead of me. I believe it could have been nesting there, and certainly the habitat then was very suitable for it. The stone curlew is a bird that once nested widely on the downs of Wiltshire, Hampshire and Sussex, but now, because of the loss of its habitat to farming, it is largely confined to the Brecklands of East Anglia. The bird requires large open spaces of rough ground, and there are plans to try and attract it back onto the Reserve. As the heathland is enlarged, the chances are good that on one spring day this migrant will be seen to settle and take up residence. By day this shy and stealthy bird is difficult to spot unless it is disturbed off its nest, which it leaves by running a few metres and then flying low over the ground. Its nest on the ground is just a shallow scrape lined with pebbles and rabbit droppings in which two eggs are laid in April and May. Night-time is when the stone curlew is most active, and its wailing voice 'coo-ree, coo-ree' is haunting and somewhat sinister when heard for the first time on a lonely heath in moonlight. Let us hope that soon its voice will once again be heard on the Downs above the Cuckmere.

A bird that used to nest in the wide expanse of gorse that covered the downs and heathlands of Southern England is the *dartford warbler*. Susceptible to cold, its numbers fell markedly in the 1960s and 1970s, when a succession of cold winters occurred. In the last few years, however, it has recovered and is now nesting regularly in Hampshire and Sussex. Plans for its reintroduction to Lullington Heath are being considered, but there is a conflict between the amount of gorse that can be allowed to grow at the expense of open heathland. The dartford warbler requires a large area of gorse, and at present the amount on the Heath could only support about one or two pairs of these delightful birds. Time alone will tell whether or not we shall see them on the Reserve.

A recent addition to the birds of the Heath is the *nightjar*. A pair of these somewhat uncommon local birds has become established in nearby Friston Forest in an open area where the trees have been felled and cleared in preparation for replanting. Now a pair, possibly offspring from the Forest, is breeding within an area of gorse on Lullington Heath itself. The nightjar is migratory, arriving from Africa in May and departing in September or October. It is seldom seen during daylight, when it sits crouched motionless along a branch or on the ground, where its mottled brown plumage gives it camouflage against a background of dead leaves and wood. Just before nightfall the male nightjar begins a remarkable nocturnal 'churring' song which lasts for as long as 15 minutes or so. The female then joins up with the male and they fly off to hunt for large moths that form the major part of their diet. The moths are caught on the wing when the nightjar's bill opens widely, revealing a huge mouth fringed with bristles which facilitate the passage of moths down their throat.

During the breeding season the birds indulge in bouts of loud 'wing clapping', which resonates across the valley on the Heath. The two white eggs blotched with brown markings, looking rather like beach pebbles, are laid on the bare ground in mid-May. The nest site, such as it is, can be under bushes, in nettles or even in the open. When the young hatch, the parents will approach you boldly and try to distract you by reeling over from side to side, often croaking loudly at the same time. Both parents look after the young, the male often finishing the task when the female commences a second brood. The nightjar is also known as the '*goat-sucker*', from a widely believed myth that, with its huge mouth, it milked goats which then went blind. There is no reason to believe that this somewhat weird but wonderful bird will not thrive and increase its numbers on the Reserve; its evening churrings and wing clapping should give pleasure to many long into the future.

The typical bird of the scrubland on the Heath is the *nightingale*. This remarkable songster arrives in Britain in April after a 6,000-kilometre journey from Central Africa. Over the last few decades the number of nightingales and other warblers in Britain has decreased alarmingly. The droughts in Africa and the drying up of much of the southern Sahara Desert as it expands southwards are the probable reasons for this, as these migrants require fresh water and insects to sustain them on their mighty journey. The best way to hear the deep bubbling and liquid notes of its enchanting song is to walk along the south side of the Heath on a still May morning just before dawn breaks. As everyone knows, the nightingale is famed for its singing throughout the night, but not everyone is aware that it sings during the day just as much. Shortly before the dawn chorus gets under way, you will hear the nightingale at its best, but it is unlikely that you will see it, since its behaviour is skulking and solitary. Look out for it, though, singing characteristically from a branch in a hawthorn thicket. The bird is somewhat featureless and inconspicuous with its almost uniform brown plumage. It builds its nest of dead leaves, lined with grass and hair, on or just above the ground, well hidden in nettles or low bushes. It is almost an impossible nest to find, but if you do accidentally come across one with its four to six olive-green eggs, do not linger in case the parents desert it.

You are almost certain to see *whitethroats* and *lesser whitethroats* anywhere on the Reserve, especially in the areas of low bushes and thickets. They again are migratory birds from Africa, arriving in April or early May, returning in September. The whitethroat is brown above and buff below, with prominent rusty-brown wings. Slightly smaller, the lesser whitethroat is of similar colour, but its wings are grey. They both nest low down in thick vegetation such as brambles and nettles. The flimsy nests are made of dry grass stems and lined with fine hair. Four to six eggs, greenish-white, spotted and speckled with grey and brown, are laid in May or June. After breeding, and a few weeks before returning to Africa, the birds tend to disperse and feed in gardens on the many insects and caterpillars to be found on cabbages and other crops. No doubt they need this nutritious and fattening diet to sustain them on their long journey south.

A bird that was once fairly common on the Heath is the *grasshopper warbler*, which looks like many of the other warblers and is usually identified by its distinctive song, which sounds just like a grasshopper or cricket 'churring'. Also likened to the winding in of an angler's reel, its song carries a long way, especially at night. The bird is by nature very skulking and secretive and creeps and runs through its habitat of thick undergrowth with great agility. It is very reluctant to fly, and not surprisingly is a bird seldom seen but often heard. In the last few years this bird has become scarcer on the Reserve, and one hopes that it will continue to survive. The nest is built, by both sexes, of strong dry grass and moss on or near the ground under gorse and other small bushes. The four to seven pale rosy-white eggs spotted with brown are laid in May and June.

Lullington Heath contains a wide range of habitats suitable for many types of birds, and a description of only a few of them can be included here. So look out for the many others, common as well as scarce, that you will see on your visit.

Butterflies are abundant, and at the right time of the year and on a bright sunny day you will see a wide variety. Almost certainly you will see a *red admiral* of the same family as the white admiral described in the previous chapter. One of our most beautiful butterflies, with its red bands and white markings on a black background, is the red admiral. Its presence in Britain depends on migrants coming across the Channel in May and laying eggs singly on the nettle plant. These hatch in a week and give rise to the familiar sight of these butterflies in the summer and autumn. If you look carefully at a patch of nettles you may see the green or brown caterpillars (there are two types) feeding on the leaves from under a 'tent' made by drawing two leaf edges together with silken threads. The chrysalis with attractive gold spots can be seen suspended from nettle stems in late summer and autumn. The butterfly itself, although a fast flyer, is easily seen except when it rests with wings folded, when its marvellously decorated underside blends in well with the vegetation. It is territorial in nature and fiercely defends its patch of hedgerow, woodland or garden by attacking and driving away intruding butterflies. You may see it sunning itself on patches of bare white chalk on paths, and in autumn look for it feasting on the juice of ripe fruit. Sadly, it cannot tolerate the cold, and does not normally survive the winter in Britain. Interestingly, in recent years there have been increasing reports of its hibernation in houses and outbuildings.

Along the south side of the Reserve, next to Friston Forest, is a path along which grows a profusion of different shrubs and flowers. This ancient Neolithic track is known as 'Snake Hill', as it is a favourite place for *adders* to sunbathe before they go off to hunt for small rodents in the scrub. The adder is Britain's only poisonous snake; its venom is a powerful heart depressant, causing rapid death of its natural prey. Humans are seldom killed by an adder bite, and there have been only about 12 fatalities in the last 60 years. If left alone, the adder will not attack humans, although on one occasion when gathering blackberries I remember being alerted to an adder's presence by a loud hissing noise. I froze, petrified, for there, only half a metre in front of me, was a large adder with its head raised about to strike me. Clearly it was concerned that I was about to step on it. Would it strike or wouldn't it? I recovered my composure and slowly, ever so slowly, walked backwards. When there was a safe distance between us, I beat a more hasty retreat. On another occasion while walking along a downland track I heard two whitethroats making a great noise with repeated and obviously agitated alarm calls. I investigated a low bush around which they were flying, and noticed to my horror a nest containing fledglings which were being devoured one by one by a fat adder. The adder had climbed up the main stem to the nest, which was about three-quarters of a metre off the ground.

The adder can be distinguished from the harmless grass snake by the black zigzag along its back and the V or X mark on the top of its head. It loves dry places and is reasonably common on the Downs, where it is most often seen in the summer months. In winter the adder hibernates, emerging only when warm days in late February or March herald the approach of spring. The females establish territories and are known to fight rivals by rearing up and pushing them away with their bodies. They mate in May, and six to twenty young are born alive in September. Over Britain as a whole, the adder population is steadily declining as more and more of our heathlands are claimed for forestation and agriculture.

Snake Hill track is a place to see the *dark green fritillary*. Recognised by the green markings and silver spots on the underneath of its wings, this quite large butterfly is a fast flyer which skims and soars between the thistle flowers which it loves. July and August are the best months to see this butterfly, which only lives for about six weeks. The female lays its eggs singly on the leaves and stem of the dog violet plant. The caterpillar hatches in 14 to 18 days, devours the eggshell and then immediately hibernates until the spring, when it emerges to start eating the leaves of its host plant. The chrysalis stage lasts for about a month and the butterflies themselves emerge in June.

Perhaps the real gem of Lullington Heath is the chalk heathland, a rare occurrence on the Downs where a slightly acidic loam covers the chalk itself. This allows acid-loving species to grow amongst those plants that favour a lime environment. I can remember in the early 1950s when a whole area of these Downs, now covered with fields of wheat, were purple with the flowers of the bell heather. Thank goodness we have saved a small portion of this unique environment as a National Nature Reserve.

The best place to see this area of heathland is in the north-east corner of the Reserve. On a clear day, the views from this high vantage point are glorious. To the south-west you look across the ever-changing colour of Friston Forest to the sparkling blue sea. To the west you view fields of corn rippling in the breeze to far-off Firle Beacon, which stands proud as one of the tallest hills on this section of the South Downs. Nearby lies the chalk heath itself, which in summer is ablaze with colour, pink and purple from the heathers and yellow from the surrounding gorse, which has its own particular smell, like coconut.

The dominant heath species is the *bell heather*, which carpets whole areas with its reddish-purple flowers shaped like small bells. The flowers, which bloom in July to September, are clustered around the end of the woody stems. Less prominent, and not so extensive, is the *ling*, which has densely packed minute leaves and small lilac-coloured flowers growing along the stems. The Latin name for ling, *calluna*, gets its name from the Greek word *kallino*, meaning to beautify. Those who have seen moorlands covered with this plant will agree with this apt name. In reality, however, the name was given because this heather was made into brooms, which did the beautifying by sweeping.

Heathers have short roots, and thus they can survive in the thin layer of acid loam over the chalk, which seldom exceeds 20 centimetres in depth. As heather dies, its remains help to increase and preserve the acidic nature of its habitat.

Another acid-loving plant growing amongst the heather here is the *tormentil*. This plant can be distinguished by its attractive four-petalled yellow flowers growing singly on long stalks. The whole plant is some 15 centimetres tall. The lower leaves grow from the woody rootstock and have stalks, but the deeply cut leaves on the stem are unstalked. The roots of tormentil contain tannin and are used in modern herbal medicine to treat the 'torments' of diarrhoea and sore throats, hence its English name. In former times the roots boiled in milk were used to treat stomach upsets in children and calves. The plant was also used to cure smallpox, cholera and whooping cough, and as a lotion for ulcers. An important plant indeed as a 'cure-all' for many ailments.

Growing prominently in the heathland is the *wood sage*, which is a stiff erect plant with a creeping rootstock and a branched stem about 30 centimetres tall. The downy leaves are toothed but undivided, and are arranged in pairs up the stem. The small pale yellow flowers are also arranged in pairs up the stems. The leaves and flowers are bitter in flavour and were used at one time as a tonic medicine and sometimes they were used as a substitute for hops in brewing.

Favouring chalky soils is the outstandingly handsome plant, the *viper's bugloss*, which grows in many parts of the Reserve, but especially along the pathways. Almost a metre high in places, its stout stems, bristling with hairs, carry attractive bell-shaped flowers in June to August which are first dark pink and then change to a bright blue. After pollination each flower produces four seeds which are said to resemble a viper's head; hence its name. For this reason also it was once used as an antidote for snakebite. With this background, not surprisingly it was also recommended as a cure for melancholy.

The viper's bugloss flowers are rich in nectar and are much frequented by sweet-tongued insects. I have seen as many as eight *burnet moths* on one plant, and what a colourful scene they made, with their red and black colours merging with the blue and pink flowers of the viper's bugloss. The burnet moth's bright colouring acts as a warning to potential predators, since if attacked they exude a yellow fluid which contains hydrogen cyanide (prussic acid). Birds who get a taste of this moth will not be tempted again! The burnet moth is not harmful to humans unless eaten. They are very common on the Downs in June and July, when they hatch out. So be careful when picnicking that they do not land on your sandwich!

Growing amongst the acid-loving plants you will find the *hound's-tongue*, which favours chalky places, and with its long tapering roots can penetrate the acid topsoil. It can be recognised by its overall greyness caused by a covering of soft, downy hairs. The flowers appear in June and July and are funnel-shaped, one centimetre across and dark crimson in colour. The leaves are long and lance-shaped, and the plant can be almost a metre tall, although those on the Reserve are usually half this size. It gives off a mousy odour and has narcotic and astringent properties.

That lovely plant the *wild thyme* can also be found growing amongst the heather. In spite of its diminutive nature, it is really a shrub with a woody rootstock that penetrates deeply. Wild thyme has a creeping stem from which arise the flowering shoots containing masses of tiny, two-lipped, rose-purple flowers which appear from May onwards, to September. The flowers contain much nectar and are highly fragrant, and consequently attract many types of insects, including, of course, the honey bee.

Two species of mignonette grow on Lullington Heath, *weld* and *wild mignonette*. You are hardly likely to miss weld, because it has a single, normally unbranched, stem about a metre and a half tall, carrying a spike of yellowish-green flowers. The undivided leaves are long and glossy. Weld is also known as *dyer's weed*, as its juice produces a beautiful yellow dye used in medieval times for dyeing wool and cotton. It is also the source of the artist's paint called 'Dutch pink'. Wild mignonette is quite distinct from weld because it is a shorter and tufted plant with deeply divided leaves. The flowers are larger and are a brighter yellow. Both plants can be found flowering from June to September.

A common plant flowering from June to August beside the pathways in grassy places is the *red bartsia*. About 30 centimetres tall, with purple-reddish flowers, red bartsia is a semi-parasitic herb whose roots attach themselves to those of other plants to derive their nourishment. The plant also feeds in the normal way as well as parasitically, hence its green colour.

More than 100 species of wild rose grow in Britain, and two of the most common ones can be found on the Heath: the dog rose and the burnet rose. The *dog rose* forms a large bush up to three metres high, with long arching branches covered with broad hooks. The leaves are made up of five leaflets which are hairless. The abundant five-petalled pink flowers blossom in June and July and result in the colourful scarlet fruits called 'hips' which adorn our hedgerows in the autumn. These hips are very rich in Vitamin C; during and just after the Second World War they were collected to produce rose-hip syrup, which was used as a nutritious food supplement. Perhaps many of you, like me, remember supplementing your pocket money by collecting rose-hips in the late 1940s and selling them for two old pence per pound to the local chemist's shop.

Less common, but I believe more attractive, is the *burnet rose*, with its small, solitary, creamy white flowers sometimes tinged with a delicate pink. Flowering from May to July, the blossoms turn into purple-black hips. Unlike those of the dog rose, the leaves are divided into seven or nine leaflets, and the whole plant forms a low-growing shrub only half a metre high.

Of the six species of orchid that grow on Lullington Heath, the most unusual and uncommon one is the *frog orchid*. Growing in the short grassland on the east side of the Reserve, this orchid can easily be missed because of its diminutive size (5–35 centimetres tall) and its overall colour of green tinged with brown. Occasionally almost the entire plant, including the flower, is a rusty-brown all over. The flowers, which appear in mid-June and continue to August, bear no resemblance to a frog, and it is difficult to understand how it got its name. Small insects act as pollinators, and the production of seed is highly efficient, which is just as well since there is no means of vegetative propagation such as by running rootstocks. The frog orchid is an orchid of chalk and limestone pastures, but its appearance is erratic. Some years on a well-known site there may be hundreds of flowers, and then it may vanish for several years. Despite the fact that there are many suitable habitats in Kent, it is very rare in that county, yet relatively common on the Sussex Downs. I wonder why this should be?

Just behind the main track in the north-west corner of the Reserve, and hidden from view by bushes, is Winchester's Pond. A typical dew-pond of indeterminate age, this small area of water is an oasis for *dragonflies*, *newts* and other aquatic wild life. It seldom dries out, and at the height of summer it is a good place to sit quietly and watch all the birds as they come to drink. I remember one hot sultry day when there was little wind and I was sitting beside the pond watching those lovely birds, *yellowhammers*, flitting from bush to bush nervously waiting to assuage their thirst. Suddenly my eye was caught by a movement at the base of a bush only some three metres away. The weasel-like head of a *wild mink* protruded through the grass. It crept quietly and stealthily to the water's edge, its rich, glossy white fur tinged with brown shining in the reflected glare of the sun. It drank for perhaps 30 seconds as I watched motionless in wonder at such a sight. Suddenly, it raised its head, looked straight at me, and without any apparent fear or fright crept slowly back into the bushes. If it saw me, it was not apparent, and I often wonder what this creature was doing so far away from its natural environment of the Cuckmere River itself. Perhaps it had found a good source of food amongst the abundant wildlife of the Reserve.

Around the edge of Winchester's Pond grow *bulrush* and *branched bur-reed*, as well as *sedges* and *rushes*. When people talk about the bulrush they generally mean *reedmace*, which is quite unmistakeable with its two rows of bluish-green leaves and well-known dark velvety-brown spike some two metres tall. The reedmace is a decorative plant in the home, and every autumn it used to be sold in London for this purpose by traders who erroneously called it bulrush. The name bulrush properly belongs to a type of club-rush which is quite unlike reedmace. The reedmace was probably misnamed because artists always portrayed their picture of Moses in the cradle surrounded by a forest of this plant which in the Bible was called bulrush.

The branched bur-reed, too, is a distinctive plant because of its large round prickly-looking flower heads which appear in June and July on branched stalks. This is an example of a plant that has separate male and female flowers on the same spike. The male flowers on the top of the spike are small and olive-coloured, while below them are the female flowers, which are much larger. The leaves of the bur-reed are long and narrow, sword-shaped, and with blunt tips.

Growing in the middle of the pond is the rare *water soldier*, which is a plant of still, lime-rich waters. Water soldier has leaves resembling those at the top of a pineapple plant, long and narrow, with sharp, saw-like edges. The plant floats on the surface in summer and puts out large white flowers four centimetres across in June to August. In Britain only female flowers are known, and therefore seeds are not produced. The plant reproduces itself by the production of offshoots that break off and float away from the main body. Unusually, after flowering, the whole plant sinks to the muddy bottom to hibernate for the winter. Nothing more is seen of the water soldier until spring, when it resurfaces, puts out fresh leaves and prepares again for flowering.

Winchester's Pond, as we mentioned earlier, is a habitat for *dragonflies*, and you will see several different species on any day in late spring and summer. Dragonflies also feed on flying insects up to the size of small butterflies, which they catch and eat in flight. Sometimes they perch to eat the large insects and then one can even hear their mandibles crunching the skeletons of their prey. Often you will see two dragonflies flying together 'in tandem' in a mating embrace. The female lays her eggs in the water, which then hatch into nymphs or larvae. These nymphs live in the water for up to two years, living off anything from tiny insects to large tadpoles, depending on the size of the nymph itself. When mature, the nymphs leave the water by climbing up plant stems in early summer. They then shed their skins and emerge as winged adults, which only live for about a month. Dragonflies are one of the fastest and oldest insects in the world, with flight speeds of up to 100 kilometres per hour. Fossilised remains show that they existed some 300 million years ago. There are 27 species of dragonfly in the British Isles, and at Winchester's Pond you are likely to see one of the *hawker dragonflies*, the *southern aeshna*, with its green and blue markings. You will also see many bright blue *damselflies*, which are smaller relatives of the dragonfly. Sit and enjoy the spectacle of these lovely flying insects with their large transparent wings as they dart around the pond with great energy and zest, carrying out many and varied antics.

As in Friston Forest, the damp days of early autumn bring a variety of fungi to the heathland. Prominent amongst these is the *parasol mushroom*, which is one of the largest British fungi, growing up to 40 centimetres tall with a cap almost 30 centimetres in diameter. It likes grassy spaces in the open, and is easily distinguished by its long, slender, scaly stem and light brown scaly cap shaped in the form of a parasol when fully developed. The gills underneath the cap are whitish, and the flesh of the cap is soft, unlike that of the stem, which is fibrous. The whole fungus has a pleasant odour, and the cap, when cooked, is delicious, with a hazelnut flavour. The stem, however, is somewhat tough. In complete contrast is the somewhat uncommon fungus called *hygrocybe* or *scarlet hood*. This small fungus has a bright scarlet bell-shaped cap some two to four centimetres across. You will find this distinctive and colourful fungus on the grassy rides that have been mowed on the heathland. Try to identify the many other species of fungi that you will find in the area by using one of the books listed in the Bibliography.

At night in the month of July pinpricks of pale yellow-green light appear on some of the grassy rides. This light comes from the luminous organs situated under the tail segments of the female *glow-worm*. To attract the male, she climbs up onto a low plant and turns onto her side, so that her underparts are directed sideways. The male glow-worm's eyes are very large and are adapted so that it can see the glow given out by the female. The male is like a beetle and can fly, but the female has no wings and is more like a beetle larva. Both sexes hide under stones and debris during the day, do not feed, and live only for about nine days. The larva of the glow-worm feeds on slugs and snails by injecting them with a digestive juice which enables it to suck up all the fluid remains.

One cannot conclude a chapter on Lullington Heath without mentioning the automated air-pollution monitoring unit. This black box, situated inside a set of black railings on the south-west corner of the Reserve near the top of Snake Hill Path, has contributed to national information on air-pollution levels since 1988. Disturbingly, in recent years it has shown that this area is one of the most polluted places in Britain for air quality. Quite difficult to believe, when on most days one can see for miles in any direction across rivers, hills, sea and open countryside. Inside the railings you will also notice a concrete cap which covers a deep shaft descending to a huge water-supply pipe which takes water from the chalk to Friston Pumping Station. The excavated soil from the shaft has made a flat area from which you can look across the whole of Lullington Heath, a marvellous vantage point. If you are very observant you will see nicks in the black railings caused by bullets when the area was a firing range and military training area in the Second World War.

How lucky we are to have as part of our heritage this veritable haven for wildlife and plants in a sea of modern agriculture. However, in the last few years a small part of this 'sea of agriculture' just outside the Nature Reserve to the north-east has been left to return to nature as part of the government's 'set-aside' scheme. Many of the formerly common cornfield plants, such as the *red poppy* and *field pansy*, have now returned. Who knows, maybe in a hundred years' time the area could once again revert to the wilderness I knew as a young boy. Let us hope so!

Kestrel

6

DEEP DENE

Deep Dene, to my mind, is one of the loneliest and most enchanting places on the South Downs. A deep coombe or valley cut out in the glacial period some 15,000 years ago, it lies just to the north-west of Lullington Heath below Windover Hill. This valley, apart from being a haven for wildlife, is steeped in history and myths. The Long Man of Wilmington, just to the north, is a famous landmark and one of the great enigmas of the chalk downs. The Long Man is of impressive size, some 65 metres tall, with slightly taller staves on either side. Originally cut directly into the chalk, his outline was given greater prominence in 1873 when white bricks were put into place. These are regularly cleaned up and repainted by volunteers. The origin of this huge figure is unknown, but local legend has it that once two giants inhabited the area, one on Windover Hill and one on Firle Beacon, some six kilometres to the west. They quarrelled, and the Windover giant was killed by a boulder thrown by the other. It is said that the dead giant was buried in the nearby long barrow or burial mound. A much more plausible story, and one that includes a possible explanation for the Long Man, is that back in the mists of time two tribal chiefs, each with their followers, inhabited the area. One tribe lived in, and controlled, the land around Firle Beacon, and the other inhabited, and controlled, Windover Hill. Between them, the Cuckmere Valley, with its ancient ford near Long Bridge, was a strategic and important locality, and the two tribes battled to gain control over this and each other's lands. One can only imagine how the battle or series of battles was fought, but eventually one or other of them won. To celebrate, the victorious tribe cut a figure of their leader in the chalk face where it could be seen for miles around. After all, we in this modern age do something very similar when a famous victory is won. We build monuments; and Nelson's statue in Trafalgar Square is but one of many examples. The staves were possibly added at a later stage as a means of identifying the easy and well-used path on top of the Downs to those struggling to find a way through the almost impenetrable woods below.

Deep Dene is very close to the point, a few hundred metres west of the Long Man, where a number of ancient trackways, including the South Downs Way, cross each other. If one stands on the top of one of the downland ridges and looks into Deep Dene, one can clearly see the 'ghosts' of circular buildings that stood there long before the Romans came. Excavation on four hut sites nearby revealed pottery of the late Bronze/early Iron Age, 500–250 BC. There are signs of a settled pastoral community living here, and the remains of a series of lynchet banks and a Celtic field system provide evidence that crops were once grown on the site. A dead-straight track cuts diagonally into the spur that runs south and to the west of Deep Dene, and this is probably of Celtic origin. Almost certainly its purpose was to provide a fast and efficient route to the ridge highway at the top for people living in Deep Dene itself. For thousands of years and many centuries ago Deep Dene was possibly a place of safety and a haven for people who lived in the small villages near the Cuckmere. They would have escaped to this secluded and heavily wooded place whenever raids from the Continent threatened.

Deep Dene is a private property, and permission to visit it should be sought from South East Water. However, a good deal of the wildlife and flora can be seen from the many public rights of way that surround it. There are three main areas to Deep Dene: the western slope, the valley bottom and the eastern slope. The western slope is still fairly open, but scrub encroachment, particularly by the *wayfaring tree*, is now becoming apparent. It is a particularly good habitat for butterflies, where its position and variety of short turf, bare patches and grasses give it a micro-climate all of its own. On windless, sunny summer days it gets extremely hot. The valley floor, with its deeper soils, is not of particular interest, but there are signs of it having once been culti-vated. The eastern slope now largely consists of tall trees, mainly ash and sycamore, and dense scrub.

There are plans to put cattle in Deep Dene to help control the spread of undergrowth and scrub, particularly the wayfaring tree. The use of cattle grazing for this purpose will be carefully managed to ensure that wildlife and plants are not adversely affected. Care will be taken to ensure that over-grazing does not occur, and I am sure that note will be taken of the recent investi-gations into the adverse effects of cowpats on plants. The hot summer of 1995 was blamed for the fact that cowpats in our fields were tougher and more long-lasting than usual. However, further investigation apparently shows that the use of an anti-parasite drug, Ivermectin, to kill worms in cattle and other livestock survives in the cowpats and kills off the beetles and bugs that normally digest and demolish them. Cowpats normally survive about 20 days, but with Ivermectin present they last as long as 60 days or more. Wild flowers have evolved to the point where they can survive under dung for a certain time, but they cannot suddenly be expected to live for two or three times that long. Particularly at risk are such plants as the *cowslip* and *squinancy-wort*. Ivermectin is cheap and powerful and is widely used by vets. Its effect on our wild flora must be thoroughly examined and if proved to be a threat its use must be carefully controlled.

Of the birds in the area, perhaps the most typical is the *kestrel*, seen hovering over the valley ready to pounce on an unwary *vole* or *fieldmouse*. You may also see one being mobbed by an angry group of noisy *jackdaws* or *rooks* that seem to delight in such activity. The kestrel wheels and dives to avoid the mob, but usually to no avail. Apart from the noise alerting the intended victims, it also affects the kestrel's concentration, which is the secret of all hunting. The kestrel gives up the unequal battle and flies off to hunt again elsewhere.

Like the sparrowhawk, the kestrel was affected by pesticides, as described in Chapter 4, but its numbers have increased consider-ably since the 1960s. It is probably the commonest of all our birds of prey and is the one familiar to people who travel at speed up and down our motorways, as it is often seen hovering over the long grass, especially at intersections. It seems oblivious and unconcerned at the traffic roaring past only a few metres away. Although its method of hunting is associated with hovering, it is also known to perch, and can sometimes be seen sitting for long periods on a telegraph pole, wire or dead branch. Obviously, hovering uses up precious energy, whereas perching does not. On the other hand, vision is somewhat limited from a perch. A whole field can easily be covered by hovering, and for this reason it is the method of hunting most often used.

The kestrel usually nests in a hole in a tree, but on many occasions it utilises the old nest of a crow or a ledge in an outbuilding. The four to seven eggs are laid at two-day intervals, commencing in March. The eggs are creamy-white, thickly blotched and clouded with reddish-brown. The female alone incubates the eggs, and after about 28 days the young hatch out. During this time the male generally brings food to the female on the nest. Sometimes he may perch nearby and call; then the female will leave the nest and receive the prey directly from him. The male's rate of hunting increases markedly after the young hatch. The young leave the nest after about 30 days, and then remain in the area for about another month. They are fed by their parents until they are strong enough on the wing to fend for themselves. An interesting fact is that the sex ratio in young kestrels is two to one in favour of the female, and yet bigamy is relatively rare in the species. This is in direct contrast to the *sparrowhawk*, where the sex ratio is roughly even, and yet bigamy and polygamy is common. More study in this area is needed to determine why this should be so.

The *magpie* commonly nests on the eastern flank of Deep Dene. This striking bird, with its black and white plumage, long tail and jerky undulating flight, is now very common and is on the increase in most areas. Beautiful it might be, but it is a menace to the small bird population in spring. Normally feeding on insects and seeds, it also robs birds of their eggs and young. The magpie is cunning and aggressive and is now a regular visitor to the suburban garden, where it thrives on the generosity and goodwill of the human species. I wonder how many people realise the immense damage a pair of these birds do to relatively unprotected garden species. There must be few of us who have not come across the broken eggshells beside the garden nest-site of a robin, blackbird, wren or hedge sparrow. Few also can not have heard the chatter of magpies in the hedges as they chase away small birds from their fledglings, which they then proceed to tear apart and devour. There are few natural predators of the magpie, and even the domestic cat has its work cut out to overcome the intelligence, sharpness of sight and sound, and speed of reaction of this bird. Even its nest is well protected, and is usually built in a thick clump of thorn bushes. It consists of a foundation of dead bramble or thorn-sticks, firmly plastered together with mud, on which is constructed an inner cup of mud lined with fine roots. A dome of thorny twigs with an entrance hole completes this large and formidable 'home', which is quite impenetrable to any potential enemy and gives good reason why the magpie is one of our more successful species.

On a still day in spring, walk along the path on the top of the eastern side of Deep Dene and listen out for the distinctive and deliberately repeated 'chiff, chaff, chiff, chaff' notes of that delightful warbler, the *chiffchaff*. It likes to sing from the top of a tall tree, so look out for it. Its song distinguishes it from the *willow warbler*, which has a more liquid musical tone to it and can also be heard in Deep Dene. Both birds are greenish-yellow and lighter underneath, but the chiffchaff has blackish legs whereas those of the willow warbler are brown. Both birds are quite small and are migratory, arriving in March from Central Africa and departing in October. Another wonder of migration when one imagines such small birds making such a long journey which they do at a never-faltering speed of 40 kilometres an hour.

The chiffchaff and willow warbler both build well-hidden, domed nests of dead leaves, grass and moss, lined with feathers or hair. The chiffchaff usually builds its nest in grass growing through bushes about 20 centimetres or so above the ground, whereas the willow warbler's nest is actually half-sunk into the ground itself and protected or hidden by grass tufts. Both species lay four to eight white eggs, spotted with pink or red, in April or May, with repeat clutches on to July. The nests, although very well concealed, can be found by watching the parent birds back either when they are building or when feeding young. But be careful and do not linger, and do not disturb the nest itself, or the birds could desert and not return.

On visits to Deep Dene in the early 1950s I can remember that there were some 15 pairs of *wheatears* nesting in rabbit burrows on the steep escarpment on the western side of the valley. I spent hours watching them as they darted to and fro about their business of building nests and feeding young. Their numbers gradually decreased until in about 1973 they disappeared altogether, and now are only infrequent visitors passing through the area. I wonder why they stopped nesting in Deep Dene?

Human disturbance could be the reason, but I question that this was the cause, as it always has been a remote and little-visited place. In any case, wheatears still seem to thrive on that much more frequented place the Seven Sisters, as described in Chapter 2.

Rabbits are certainly not disappearing in Deep Dene; quite the reverse. On the western slope and at the north end of the valley they are much in evidence. Rabbits live in colonies and construct a maze of burrows to form a warren. Breeding may occur throughout the year, but mainly takes place between January and June. The female rabbit, or doe, as she is known, digs a separate burrow, which she lines with grass and fur. She can produce a litter of between three and six young every month, but in reality this does not occur. On average a doe will produce ten live young per year. The young stay below ground for a week or so, being suckled daily by their mother; she blocks off the entrance when she leaves, to protect it against enemies and to conserve heat. The young are able to fend for themselves after a month, and they can breed themselves after about three or four months. However, their mortality rate is high, and on average adults themselves rarely live more than a year. Rabbits usually feed at dawn and dusk, and will eat up to 500 grams of fresh green food a day, be it grass, leaves, young trees or bark. This food is partly digested and excreted in the form of soft, moist pellets, which are immediately eaten again and fully digested, emerging as the hard dry pellets we see lying on the ground. There is no doubt that too many rabbits in one area is harmful to vegetation and wild plants. Too often a site of rare plants has to be protected from the ravages of the rabbit, and in many places where they have complete freedom they maintain a grass sward so shallow that only dwarf plants can survive.

Amongst the woodland area and on the top slope of the valley you will find the large irregular shaped entrances to *badger* setts. These setts or underground homes are dug out by the badger, using its short, powerful legs and strong claws. The entrances are easily spotted because of the amount of excavated earth and stones that build up in front and below it. It is interesting to note the number of *lesser burdock* plants that grow near the entrances here at Deep Dene, possibly caused by the badger brushing the clinging bur-covered seed heads off their fur before entering the sett. The tunnel to the chamber where the family lives is some 10 to 18 metres long. The chamber is kept very clean, and fresh bracken, leaves and grass are brought in by the female, or sow, as she is called, during night excursions from the sett. Badgers are fairly common throughout Britain and are related to the stoat and weasel. They are nocturnal and seldom seen during the day and have no natural enemies except man. Dusk is possibly the best time to observe them as they leave their sett with their characteristic ambling gait. Under the cover of darkness they roam far and wide across the countryside, and with their acute sense of smell they feed on anything from worms, mice, frogs and young rabbits to blackberries and windfall fruit. The badger particularly likes wasps' nests containing grubs and eggs, and with its thick skin covered with hair is quite indifferent to wasps angrily buzzing about it and their stings. The badger digs and scrapes until the nest is licked clean, and then goes off to look for another.

At the first hint of dawn the animals make their way back home. They do not get lost, because they mark their trails by squatting at various points on their route so that the scent from their anal glands is left behind. Their territories are marked in this way, too. Badgers wear conspicuous paths that radiate from their setts, and these are often mistaken for footpaths. Often I have followed one of these, only to be blocked when the trail disappears below a low bush. Badgers mate any time between February and October, but the fertilised egg does not start developing until December. One to five cubs are born usually in February, and these live with their parents until autumn, when they leave to establish new homes for themselves.

If you have patience, walk up to Deep Dene on a warm summer evening, sit quietly a few metres away from a sett which you can tell is occupied from the evidence of fresh earth and characteristic black and white pieces of fur that lie about it. As the sun dips below the rim of the Downs and your eyes become accustomed to the dark, you will soon hear the soft scraping sound of a badger coming out of its sett. Studies have shown that badgers emerge about 20 to 90 minutes after the sun sets, the time corresponding to the season; 20 minutes around 21 June and 90 minutes in mid-December. Clearly the amount of actual night-time available to feed is important. You should get a glimpse of these lovely animals as they emerge. Sit downwind of the sett; the badger may not even sense you are there, and you will see it shuffle off into the darkness. If you are upwind of the sett it will quickly smell you, and your only sight of it will be a striped snout at the entrance and then no more as it backs down into the tunnel. Enjoy your badger-watching!

There are 120 different species of *snails* in Britain, and you are certain to see some of these just about anywhere. Snails live in their 'whorled' home or shell, which is made of chalk. Snails move slowly and generally feed on plants, fruits and decaying matter. They have a large area in their intestine where a huge amount of food can be ingested. This can then be digested at leisure from the safety of their hideaway under stones, logs or leaf-litter. They can go for a long time without food, but they do need water to maintain the moisture in their bodies. For this reason they are nocturnal animals, emerging when the nights are damp with dew or rain. In dry weather they retreat into their shells and plug the aperture. Snails can live up to ten years, but most die within two years, notably after they have spawned eggs. The white and almost translucent eggs are laid in batches under stones or in the soil.

Two species which you will find anywhere around Deep Dene are the *white-lipped banded snail* and the *common* or *garden snail*. The white-lipped banded snail is about 15 millimetres tall and is white with dark brown stripes. It is said that sheep are very fond of eating this snail, and this gives South Downs mutton its special flavour! The garden snail is large, some four centimetres high, and is cream-coloured with brown streaks; it is common all over the chalk Downs. A similar but rare species is the *Roman snail*, which is said to have been introduced by the Romans as an item for their table furnishings. The Roman snail is edible and is favoured by the French, but I have not yet tried him in that role!

Deep Dene, with its chalk grassland slopes and rich variety of plant life, is noted for the number of butterfly species that inhabit it. Of these, the *grayling*, the largest of the brown butterfly family, is perhaps the most striking. Unlike most of the brown butterflies, it is a powerful flyer with a wingspan of five centimetres and inhabits the Downs and heathlands near the coast. It is coloured brown on top, with silver-brown splashes and two prominent 'eye-spots'; underneath, it is very inconspicuous, with a colouring of silver-grey. When it first alights on ground or grass with its wings closed, it is fairly conspicuous because of the two white-centred eye-spots on its fore-wings. These fore-wings are quickly retracted, however, and then the butterfly is hard to see. If the sun is shining, the grayling will craftily tilt over sideways into the sun so that no revealing shadow is cast. The courtship display of the grayling is fascinating. The smaller male takes up a regular obser-vation post on the ground and then flies up to inspect every butterfly that passes, even if it is not a female grayling. When a female grayling is intercepted, the male follows, and if she settles then he settles nearby. He then approaches her. If she walks away flapping her wings, he ignores her, but if she remains motionless then he commences a complex display in front of her. This display consists of rapid wing movements, opening and closing and fanning, often touching those of the female and her antennae. This is combined with movements of the body, circling around the female. Finally, mating takes place and eggs are laid singly on grass in July and August. The caterpillars hatch in some two weeks, feed on grass and then hibernate for the winter. Feeding recommences in spring, and the adult butterflies emerge from their chrysalids in July and August – they live for only three to four weeks.

Graylings seem fond of alighting on one's bare arms or legs, and I remember one hot dry July day on the western slope of Deep Dene when two did just this. They seemed oblivious of each other and me, and were reluctant to leave. Even when gently pushed off my leg they soon returned. I believe they sought the moisture and body salts from my skin. Occasionally you will find small red mites attached to the body of the grayling. These mites, which are associated with dung, suck the body fluid out of the butterfly and eventually kill it. They can be found on just about any butterfly species.

Another butterfly commonly seen here is the *small skipper*. There are eight species of skipper butterflies, and they get their name from their darting flight pattern and fast wing-beat. The small skipper, with a wingspan of three centimetres, is orange-brown on top with a black edge around it. The male can be distinguished from the female because it has a prominent black line of scent scales on the top of each fore-wing. The small skipper favours long grass where there are plenty of wild flowers such as scabious, thistles and knapweed. The eggs are laid on grasses in batches of three to five and hatch in three weeks. The caterpillars feed on the grasses and hibernate during the winter, protecting themselves from predators by making a small cocoon and pulling the sides of a grass leaf around it. They continue feeding in spring and form chrysalids in May. The adult butterflies emerge to fly in June to August. They live for only about 20 days, and you will need great patience to study them because they are very alert and are difficult to follow.

Flying with the small skipper around Deep Dene is the *Essex skipper*, which is very similar. Until 1888 this butterfly was unknown, although it had probably existed in Britain for thousands of years. In that year a collector in Essex identified a new species of skipper which had a black tip on the underside of each antenna, instead of the small skipper's yellow tip. Further studies showed that the eggs of this new species, named the Essex skipper, overwinters as an egg and not as a caterpillar. This fact was important during the 1953 floods; its eggs survived, but the caterpillars of many other species did not. You will need good eyesight to distinguish between these two skippers, but you will enjoy the challenge. So persevere, and good hunting!

One of the rare butterflies to be found here is yet another skipper, the *silver-spotted skipper*. This butterfly can be distinguished from the previous two skippers by the beautiful green and silvery-white markings on the undersides of its hindwings. The silver-spotted skipper is found in only a few sites in southern England, and requires a certain type of habitat. Short chalk grassland with a south-facing slope giving plenty of sunshine is preferred. Sadly, over the years the plough has destroyed much of such areas in Britain. This, together with the spread of scrubland over many otherwise suitable places, has led to the decline of a species already on the northern limits of its range. The life cycle of the silver-spotted skipper is similar to that of the small skipper. However, its caterpillar has evolved an unusual and fascinating habit. It feeds on grasses, and when it feels the hot breath of a grazing animal it immediately curls up and drops to the ground, where it escapes the danger of being eaten.

One cannot leave Deep Dene's butterflies without a mention of one of the several species of blue butterfly that fly in the area, namely the *Adonis blue*. The male Adonis blue is the brightest and most vivid blue of all British butterflies, and is, quite aptly, named after Adonis, the god of masculine beauty. The female is not so adorned and is brown in colour, with just a hint of blue where the wings come out from the body. Both sexes have a chequered white band around all the wings. The eggs are laid singly on the underside of the horseshoe vetch leaf in May and again in August. They hatch after about 30 days and the caterpillars, which are green with yellow stripes, feed on the host plant only at night. The summer caterpillars live for about two months before becoming chrysalids. After some three weeks these chrysalids turn into adult butterflies. The later caterpillars hibernate throughout the winter, form chrysalids in April and develop into butterflies in May. There are, therefore, two generations of this butterfly, one flying in May and June and the other in August and September. The Adonis blue requires certain types of plant, such as vetches and marjoram, to feed on, and, like the silver-spotted skipper, it needs a specific type of habitat, i.e. a chalk grassland slope facing south or south-west. These are now hard to find, and consequently the Adonis is a declining species which requires specific conservation efforts, such as scrub clearance, to enable it to survive. Thank goodness this has been recognised and these efforts are being made by bodies such as South East Water in conjunction with English Nature.

Conservation efforts are also planned to increase the presence of the rare *wart-biter cricket* in the country. This large green cricket can be found on another English Nature Reserve in the county, and there are plans to introduce it to Deep Dene. This insect, said to have been used long ago to remove warts, has definite habitat requirements. Long grass is needed for concealment, and short turf is also necessary to obtain heat from the sun's rays. Gaps in the turf are required for the female to lay her eggs in. These essential habitat characteristics can all be met at Deep Dene, and I am sure that soon after this book is published this attractive insect will be well installed and thriving.

The plant life of the area is not as prolific as Lullington Heath, the main reason being that the chalk heathland is absent. However, a good variety of wild flowers can be found in and around Deep Dene at almost any time from early spring to late autumn.

Take a walk along the slopes at the end of March, and on the rough ground at the head of the valley you will find *spring whitlow-grass*, one of the smallest and earliest of our flowering plants. From three to eight centimetres tall, the flowering stem rises from a little rosette of toothed lance-shaped leaves. The stems bear minute, white, four-petalled flowers which bloom from March to June. In medieval times this plant was supposed to have been used to cure painful lumps known as 'whitlows'; hence its name.

On some of the many anthills that abound in the area you may discover the bright blue flowers of another tiny plant, the *early forget-me-not*, which flowers from March to June. The whole plant is only about two to three centimetres tall, and the flowers themselves are only about three millimetres in diameter. Although it can be found growing on the dry grassy banks around Deep Dene, it seems to prefer the soft mossy mounds of the *yellow hill ant*'s nest. Why this should be so is a mystery to me, but you will also see *wild thyme*, mentioned in the last chapter, flourishing on these anthills of the chalk Downs. Perhaps these plants obtain some substance that is a by-product of this ant's activities. It is a known fact that over a period of time the soil of which the yellow hill ant builds its nest becomes more acid than the surrounding earth, and perhaps this is an explanation.

The yellow hill ants of the Downs are only one of 47 species of

British ants. They live in a network of tunnels dug out of the rich topsoil of the chalk. These form dome-shaped nests or mounds which look like molehills and cover the chalk slopes. The shape of the mounds is interesting, because they nearly always have a slope leading up to the highest point which then falls at a sharp angle to form a steep face. The nests contain large colonies from only 100 or so to 100,000 individuals, and they can last for more than 50 years.

The yellow hill ant feeds almost solely on the excretions of aphids, but occasionally it will eat the flesh of other insects. The ant keeps aphid eggs in its nest throughout the winter and in the spring it puts the newly hatched aphids out to 'graze' on the roots of plants growing on its nest.

At least one queen ant lives in each nest, and she does little else other than lay eggs. Each egg goes through a pupa stage. Most hatch out into sterile, wingless workers who nest-build, organise the food and defend the site. The remainder develop into queens and males, both of which have wings. On a summer's day, the queens and males fly off from the nest for their 'marriage flight'. Hundreds fill the air in great swarms, and the queens are each fertilised by several males. The queens then either return to their old nest or start up a new one. The life histories and habits of our ant population is fascinating and complex. Their 'slaves', their relationships with other insects and their overall organisation is worth a study all of its own. No wonder their workings have sometimes been compared to those of human society.

On the dry valley slopes one of our most exotic orchids, the *bee orchid*, can be found. The bee orchid is widely distributed in Britain, favouring chalk grasslands, although it is also known to flower on stabilised sand dunes and on clay soils. It flowers from June to August. The flower spike, carrying two to seven flowers, ranges in height from 15 to 30 centimetres, and arises from a rosette of greyish-green oblong lance-shaped leaves. These base leaves, like those of the early spider orchid, can be found as early as February, often with their edges burnt brown by frost. The leaves on the spike are much narrower and sword-shaped, and clasp the stem. The flower itself has a remarkable resemblance to a bumble-bee, with a broad brown furry lip with deep yellow markings. Around this lip are three pink sepals, each with a delicate green line down the middle. The bee orchid is self-fertile and does not need insects to pollinate it. This has been proved by placing a net over the plant, to exclude insects while admitting the wind. All the flowers developed full seed-pods.

However, the bee orchid does produce hybrids between itself and other similar orchids such as the spider orchid, so there must still be some cross-fertilisation by insects. Many botanists have attempted to explain the likeness of the flower to a bee. Some have said the purpose is to attract bees to provide cross-fertilisation, others have said that because the flowers are self-fertile, the purpose is to keep off bees by giving the impression that one was in occupation already. An intriguing explanation has been suggested that the bee replica discourages cattle from eating the orchid. Whatever the explanation, we are left with a plant species that is certainly worth finding, just to sit and ponder on the processes of evolution that produced such loveliness and symmetry.

In various places in the valley bottom, look out for the tall woolly plant of *great mullein*. The flower spike is some 120 centimetres high and carries many clusters of yellow flowers, which bloom from June to August. The leaves at the base of the plant are very large, sword-shaped and covered with soft, wool-like hairs. Our Saxon forefathers dipped the dried stems and flower heads in melted grease and then used them as torches at medieval church festivals. Before the introduction of cotton, the leaves and stem were used as lamp wicks. The leaves are also used in homeopathic medicine as a tincture to ease coughing. The whole plant, including the flowers, has soothing properties and has been used over the centuries in many medicinal concoctions to ease such ailments as asthma, nervousness, neuralgia and stomach cramp.

Two plants flowering in late summer and autumn are the *carline thistle* and the *yellow toadflax*. Both favour the dry banks and field borders beside the trackways that cross the valley. The carline thistle is a very spiny plant with deeply lobed leaves, growing from 5 to over 30 centimetres tall. It could not be called a beautiful plant, but the form of its leaves, its spiny nature and straw-coloured flowers give it a striking appearance. In dry weather the spiky 'petals' surrounding the flower heads (they are actually bracts, not petals) open flat, but in damp conditions they curve over the flower heads in a protective cover. The whole plant has an 'everlasting' texture and appearance, and in winter, long after the flowering period is over, you will still see it standing out amongst the dead grasses and vegetation that surround it. If cut and placed indoors it will retain its form and appearance for years.

The yellow toadflax is easily recognised from afar by its bright yellow long-spurred flowers with their 'snapdragon' appearance. If you gently press the sides of the flower, the lips will part, disclosing its reproductive organs, the stamens (male) and pistil (female). Only powerful insects, such as the honey bee or bumble-bee, can exert sufficient force to open the lips and obtain the honey contained in the long hollow spur. Even long-tongued bees must thrust their heads well into the flower to reach the honey, and in doing so brush their backs against the pollen on the stamen and fertilise the pistil. Sometimes the bee is crafty, and to save time and effort it bites a hole in the spur from outside and so gets at the honey without rendering the plant any service whatsoever. Occasionally you will find flowers with such holes in their spurs. Eventually, I suppose, natural selection and evolution will ensure that some development takes place to prevent such reprehensible conduct on the part of the bee.

How does one leave Deep Dene, with its ghosts of history, its loneliness and its peace and quiet? Visit it, as I once did, just before sunset on a still evening in November. Sit on a high vantage point looking down the valley to the sea shining with the reflected light of the low sun. Only the bark of a fox echoing below breaks the profound silence. Mist begins to form as the wind sweeps up the downland slopes. On the hillside in the near distance you will see all the mellow colours of autumn: the pale green and golden yellow of ash and sycamore trees before leaf-fall, and the splashes of orange and red of berries on the bushes. The wild clematis, too, straggling over the hawthorn, shows up as clumps of silver-white caught by the sun as it drops down to the horizon of the sea. Before you indeed lies a kaleidoscope of colours whose memory will sustain you in the dark winter days to come.

Long-Tailed Tit

7

AROUND CRADLE HILL

Just to the north of the public car park at High-and-Over there is a track which leads over the crest of Cradle Hill to Camp Hill and beyond. Walk this path to Bostal Hill and Bopeep Chalk Pit, some five kilometres away on the northern escarpment of the South Downs, and you will be rewarded by fine views of deep valleys, grassland slopes and fascinating areas of thicket, wood and scrub. All contain a remarkable variety of birds, plants and insects. Much of this area was saved for the nation by the National Trust, which purchased it in 1991 with money from bequests, donations, local appeals and a Countryside Commission grant.

This chapter will concentrate on the natural history around Cradle Hill to the north and west of High-and-Over. The area is dominated by a fine downland slope which stretches from the main Alfriston to Seaford road for a kilometre or so before it turns northwards and ends up as a mass of cultivated fields near Bostal Bottom. The most interesting part is the area around Cradle Hill and Camp Hill, just to the west. The escarpment here is ancient chalk grassland with its wonderful flora and insect life. Just below the path at the bottom is an area which many years ago was cultivated land but has been allowed to return to nature. Wild orchids have begun to grow on it again, but it will be many years before its transformation back to rich grassy downland is complete. Camp Hill is just outside the National Trust area, but it is well worth visiting. The name Camp Hill and its associated track called Comp are associated with the Roman word describing uncultivated land on the edge of a villa estate. This is not surprising, because much of the area is steeped in Roman and pre-Roman antiquity. Indeed, just to the west and on the path to Bostal Hill mentioned earlier, there are some burial mounds known as Five Lord's Burgh, where five manors are said to have met. There are many public footpaths of ancient origin in the area; but try taking the one that leads north up to Cross Dyke and the picturesque valley of France Bottom and Short Bottom, for there you will get some breath-taking views. Wherever you go in this area, you will find many places where solitude, peace and wide open spaces will be your only companion.

Of the bird life in the area, perhaps the *long-tailed tit* is one of the more interesting examples to start with. Unmistakeable with its very long tail and white crown-striped head, this bird is often heard before it is seen. Its voice has a distinctive low 'tupp' sound, with repeated trilling 'tsirrup' and a weak 'tzee-tzee-tzee'. Where you hear one, there will probably be several others, as these engaging and sociable birds hunt together in family parties, looking for insects and grubs as they flit amongst the leaves of trees and bushes. The long-tailed tit is a master builder, skilfully constructing a beautifully camouflaged domed nest in a thorn bush or patch of brambles. The nest is covered with cobwebs and lichens and lined with huge numbers of feathers; as many as 2,000 have been counted in one nest alone. You will be lucky to find one of these carefully hidden nests which blend in so well with their surroundings. However, you may spot the parent bird carrying material as it starts to build its nest as early as February. The seven to twelve eggs are laid in March or April, with repeat clutches in May and June. The tiny eggs are white, with faint red or reddish-brown spots. One of the marvels of this bird is how the parents incubate and rear so large a family in such a small nest. But succeed they do, the male keeping the female company in the nest at night during the brooding period. The large brood possibly helps the species to survive as the birds are frail and very susceptible to a cold and prolonged winter. Their numbers were reduced markedly in the winter of 1963, but since then they have increased steadily and are now a common bird of the countryside and garden.

The *great tit* is another bird you will most certainly see. It has a distinctive glossy blue-black head and neck, with yellow underparts and a black band down the centre. The voice of the great tit is very varied, but if you hear the sound of a saw cutting through wood then it is almost certainly this bird. This, the largest of our eight tit species, is aggressive and a bully, and has been known to kill and peck out the brains of smaller birds. Great tits nest typically in a hole in a tree from about one to fifteen metres above ground. It also takes readily to nest boxes, as does its smaller counterpart the *blue tit*. Great tits often return year after year to the same hole to breed. The nest itself is made of dry grass and moss, lined with hair, wool and feathers, and the parent bird is easily watched back to its nest site during its construction. The five to ten eggs, which are white, spotted and freckled with pale red, are laid from April to June. The young (and there could be up to ten of them) spend about 20 days in the nest, by which time they have consumed some 7,000–8,000 caterpillars – the parent birds are kept very busy supplying each young about 40 caterpillars a day.

As I write, some interesting research has just been published about the great tit. Data collected over the last 40 years has shown that the weight of the great tit increased as the sparrowhawk population decreased in the 1950s due to pesticides. As the numbers of sparrowhawks increased in the 1970s, following tighter regulations governing pesticide use, so the great tit has become leaner and thus more agile. Clearly, they are somehow able to assess the risks of being attacked by a predator and respond physiologically. During the autumn all small birds fatten themselves up to survive the winter, but they also need to stay slim to elude the sparrowhawk, especially at this time when vegetative cover is reduced. So a compromise must be reached between these conflicting requirements.

Another bird you are likely to see and hear is the *yellowhammer*. One of the five species of buntings resident in Britain, the yellowhammer is easily recognised by its yellow head and underparts and chestnut-brown upper surface, which are especially bright in the springtime. Perched on a bush, it sings lustily a song sounding just like 'a-little-bit-of-bread-and-no-che-ee-se'. In early April you may be lucky to see the courtship display; the male chases after the female, which is slightly duller in appearance, in a series of twisting flights that end up with them falling onto the ground, where they mate. Occasionally you may see the male bird parade around the female with spread wings and tail and erect crest. They nest typically on the ground in a bank or base of a bush or hedge, the nest being made of grass and moss, lined with hair and finer grass. The three to six eggs are laid from April to as late as August, and are ashy-white and curiously marked with dark purple as if a child had scribbled all over them. This characteristic once gave the bird its country name of '*scribbling lark*'. Yellow-hammers feed mainly on the ground, hopping and pecking as they go at seeds and leaves. They also take worms and insects and are very fond of blackberries.

Amongst the bushes and small trees on the steep slope of Cradle Hill you will come across the *wood pigeon*. The largest of the five species of pigeon in this country, the wood pigeon is distinctive with its broad white patches on the side of its neck and white band across its wings. Wood pigeons are one of the farmers' enemies because they are so destructive to crops, feeding on grain and green food such as cabbages, clover and young corn. The wood pigeon's nest is a lattice of small twigs woven into a loose platform placed in the branches of bushes or trees some 2 to 20 metres above the ground. The two white eggs are laid any time from March to September. While walking along the quiet paths shaded and covered completely in places by overhanging bushes, I have many times been startled by a wood pigeon 'exploding' out of a bush or tree with a clatter of wings. Looking carefully at the place from which the bird emerged, I have often found the nest and eggs. The nest is seldom well concealed and can easily be seen through the branches. The young hatch out after about 17 days and are fed by both adults with a protein-rich, cheese-like 'milk' which is produced in the bird's crop. The wood pigeon is the only bird that produces such a milk, similar to that of a mammal.

The *pheasant* is another bird that occasionally alarms one, when it suddenly flies up out of the grass nearby with a flapping of wings and a loud cackle. This unmistakeable and, in the case of the male, beautiful bird can be seen just about anywhere in the area, either along the tracks through the bushes or, more commonly, amongst the grass at the bottom of the downland slopes. Pheasants were probably introduced by the Romans, whose original stock came from the Caucasus; but later introductions from eastern China have meant that the wild British pheasant stock is now largely composed of many hybrids. A much sought-after bird for the table, the pheasant is now reared by many farmers in woods under carefully controlled conditions. The true wild pheasant – and thank goodness there are still many of them – is a shy bird that can often be heard when its strident double note 'koork-kok' echoes from a wood on a still midwinter's day. Pheasants are ground-dwelling birds, and their nests are carefully concealed, often in long grass under the shelter of hedges or fallen branches. The nest itself is just a scrape in the ground, lined with

Plate 19   Yellow Water Lily or Brandy Bottle, Page 107   D. L. Vinall

Plate 20   Chicory, Page 39   Author   Plate 21   White Helleborine, Page 39   Author

Plate 22   Female Whitethroat, Page 48   M. Hollings

Plate 23   Male Whitethroat, Page 48   M. Hollings

Plate 24   Pheasant's Eye, Page 38   Author

Plate 25   Silver-Spotted Skipper, Page 68   Author

Plate 26   Red Admiral, Page 49   Author

Plate 27   Red Admiral, Page 49   Author   Plate 28   Branched Bur-reed, Page 55   Author

Plate 29   Parasol Mushroom, Page 56   Author   Plate 30   Bee Orchid, Page 70   Author

Plate 31   Badger foraging, Page 64   M. Hollings

Plate 32   Carline Thistle, Page 71   H. M. Proctor

Plate 33   Wild Clematis at Deep Dene, Page 72 and 84   Author

Plate 34   Marbled White, Page 78   Author

Plate 35   Cowslips, Page 81   Author

Plate 36   Pyramidal Orchid, Page 83   Author   Plate 37   White Pyramidal Orchid, Page 83 Author

Plate 38   Orange Tip, Page 95   D. L. Vinall

grass, leaves and feathers. The 10 to 15 olive-brown eggs are laid from April to June and hatch out after about 25 days. Sometimes the same nest will be shared by two hen birds and as many as 20 or so eggs will be found in the nest. The pheasant's eggs and young are very vulnerable to foxes, weasels, stoats and other predators, and concealment and camouflage are essential for their survival. Usually only three or four young will survive to adulthood. Occasionally one will come across a hen pheasant with her young brood furtively crouching in the grass, their mottled buff and grey colours blending in perfectly with their surroundings.

As you walk along the track bordering cultivated fields, a *common partridge* may suddenly rise close by with rapidly whirring wings and calling excitedly 'kri-kri-kri'. The common partridge is a very plump bird with a small rounded head, tiny bill and brown and grey plumage. It thrives on cultivated land, where it feeds on the grain of wheat, oats and barley. It also feeds on weed seeds and is often seen on newly ploughed fields, where it pecks for worms and insects. Changes in agricultural practice over the years have had their effect on the partridge's way of life. When reaping was done by hand and corn was left to dry in rough bundles on fields, many seeds were left scattered on the ground. With the advent of modern machinery such as the combine harvester, practically no seeds are left over, and even the remaining stubble is now quickly ploughed in. Other changes have taken place. Crop rotation, with some fields left fallow, was once the dominant form of agriculture, and this provided an abundance of insect life. This practice has long died out, leaving less cover and feed for the partridge. Again, farming practice has allowed many of our hedgerows to be grubbed up so that larger and larger areas can be used for crops. Hedgerows always provided the partridge with good cover and plenty of good nesting sites. So this bird, in many parts of eastern England especially, has been driven more and more into the open, with the result that more eggs are destroyed by agricultural machinery when it tries to nest in crops, and the sitting bird falls a much easier victim to the fox and other predators.

But in this area around Cradle Hill we are lucky that the National Trust has preserved such a good habitat for this bird. Here the common partridge will nest in similar places to the pheasant, in tufts of long grass beside and just underneath bushes. The nest itself is just a few blades of dry grass in which the 10 to 16 pale olive-brown eggs are laid in May and June. These hatch in about 25 days and the young chicks leave the nest after only a few hours. They are able to fly after about 14 days and then become less vulnerable to the fox, weasel and stoat. Let us hope that this delightful game bird continues to thrive – and to give us one of the most delightful sounds of the countryside when on a warm summer's evening its call of 'kâr-wit, kâr-wit, kâr-wit' can be heard in the quiet valleys of the Downs.

From near the top of one of the paths leading down from Camp Hill, you can look across the valley over the Pumping Station to a small chalk pit in the middle of a field on the opposite slope. At one time this would have provided chalk to spread over fields to maintain their fertility and prevent them from becoming too acid. Now the advent of fertilisers has made its use obsolete, and it has reverted to nature. With binoculars, you will see the colours of many wild flowers conspicuous against the white of the chalk. You may get a glimpse of stonechats and wheatears, and you will almost certainly see a series of green tracks that radiate from the pit and out across the field to nearby woods and thickets. Undoubtedly they are the tracks of a fox which has made its home in the soft earth near the entrance to the chalk pit.

With its amber eyes, black-tipped ear, golden red coat and long full tail, the *fox* is truly a beautiful creature. The fox makes its den or earth by digging a hole under a tree root or by enlarging a rabbit warren. It can also occupy and utilise part of a badger's sett. A fox's earth is untidy, smells musky and often has food remains and excrement left around it; quite unlike that of the tidy and clean badger. The male (or dog-fox) and female (or vixen) spend solitary lives for most of the year, but they come together in winter to mate, and the three to six young are born in March or April. The young quickly learn to hunt and fend for themselves, and within two or three months they leave the earth to lead their own lives. The fox with its acute sense of smell generally hunts at night, utilising the well-marked tracks it has made for itself. It will eat just about anything it can catch, from rabbits, its staple diet, to hedgehogs, rats and birds. In the depths of winter, or when times are hard, it will even eat insects such as beetles. With a good deal of patience and by sitting downwind of a fox's den, you may be lucky enough to see one emerge and with careful, stealthy steps proceed to stalk some feeding rabbit.

June, July and August are the best months for butterflies, and on a hot sunny day the slopes below Cradle Hill can be swarming with marbled whites, meadow browns and chalkhill blues.

Despite its name, the *marbled white* is one of the brown family of butterflies and is really a black butterfly with white spots rather than a white butterfly with black spots. Two hundred years ago this butterfly was known as the *half-mourner*, because women then wore black and white dresses during the period of 'half-mourning' which followed full mourning for a dead relative. Its name then changed to *marmoress*, meaning 'marble-like', and finally about a hundred years ago it became known as the marbled white. This butterfly is often extremely abundant on the slopes in June and July, when its contrasting colours make it very conspicuous as it feeds on flowers with its wings wide open. The greater knapweed and field scabious are two of its favourite plants. The female, which is slightly larger than the male, does not attach her eggs to a leaf but scatters them amongst the grasses while in flight. The caterpillars hatch in about 18 days, feed on grass and then hibernate over winter to resume feeding in February or March. The chrysalis is formed in June and the butterfly hatches out about 25 days later.

Another of the brown butterfly family to be found here in great quantities is the *meadow brown*, one of the commonest and most widespread of our butterflies. The female is larger than the male and unusually is more brightly coloured as well. This is in contrast to most butterfly species, where the male is the more colourful. The meadow brown has a single prominent false eye on each fore-wing on both the underside and upperside. These false eye-spots stand out well against the orange and brown wing colours and are said to confuse predatory birds. Birds will tend to peck at these spots rather than the real eyes, thus allowing the butterfly to escape with just a damaged wing. All of the browns have such false eye-spots, each with a greater or lesser degree of prominence. Even on a dull day, when all the other species are dormant and hiding away, the meadow browns will rise up out of the long grass and fly around in front of you. The female lays her eggs singly on grass stems in summer, and these hatch out into green and yellow caterpillars after about two to three weeks. The caterpillars feed on grasses at night during mild spells throughout the winter. They form pale green chrysalids with black stripes at the base of grass stems in May and June, from which the adult butterflies emerge after about a month. Like most butterflies, the meadow brown has a short lifespan of only three or four weeks.

Not to be missed on the grassy slopes in July is the sight of large numbers of that beautiful butterfly the *chalkhill blue*. The male is a bright silvery blue with dark markings around the wings and is much more colourful than the darker and somewhat drab female. This colour difference is probably to help the male to attract females and to conceal the female from predators. Both sexes have a white edge to the wings and a row of spots on the hind-wings, orange in the female and black in the male. The chalkhill blue is a local species that is only found where either the horseshoe vetch, kidney vetch or bird's-foot trefoil grow, for it is on these plants that the eggs are laid in late August and on which the pale green hairy caterpillars emerge to feed some nine months later.

If you have great patience, then find one of these caterpillars, and with your hand lens watch it for awhile. You may be lucky enough to witness a remarkable sight of mutual co-operation in the world of nature. Watch for *ants* climbing onto the back of the caterpillar, not to attack it, but to stimulate a porous gland which then secretes a sweet fluid. This fluid, rich in nutrients, provides food for the ants. The caterpillar's reward comes later when it turns into a chrysalis in June. At the base of the food plant, the ants now construct a hideaway and place of safety for the chrysalis, made up of small pieces of chalk and other debris. They then keep guard over their 'charge' until it hatches out into an adult butterfly about a month later. This butterfly used to be quite common on the chalk downs of southern England, but the ploughing up of many of the grasslands and the encroachment of scrub has meant a reduction of its food source, and thus of the Chalkhill blue itself. However, the advent of National Nature Reserves and their associated resources management has allowed this beautiful butterfly not only to survive but to increase in areas where it has a foothold.

As you walk through the shady glades on the edges of the downland copses, you will almost certainly see the *ringlet* butterfly. With an overall colour of very dark brown, it derives its name from the string of false eyes on the underside of the wings, three on each fore-wing and five on each hind-wing. The ringlet is the only British butterfly with so many prominent false eye-spots. The female, which is lighter in colour and larger than the male, scatters her eggs amongst the grasses in flight in a similar fashion to the marbled white. The light brown caterpillars hibernate in grasses in winter, only feeding on mild nights. They resume continual feeding in March to form chrysalids in June. These turn into adult butterflies after about two weeks. The ringlet is a common species that may not look at first sight to be very attractive. However, watch it as it feeds on the nectar of bramble flowers, and, as the sun's rays filtering through the leaf canopy catch the wings and its false eyes, then it becomes a delicate creature of loveliness and fascination.

You will see many other species of butterfly during your walks in the area, so do take an identification guide with you. Make a note of the approximate numbers seen and the date. You can compare these on future visits, and this will provide a useful guide to their well-being or otherwise.

Thanks to conservation work, scrub encroachment of the rich grassland slopes in the area of Cradle Hill has been kept under control, allowing a profusion of wild flowers to grow.

'Where have all the cowslips gone?' is an expression now commonly heard from people in any discussion of conservation or natural history. I remember walking these hills of the South Downs 40 years ago on bright April days, and just about anywhere I would see a host of *cowslips* scattered over the slopes showing up as patches of rich yellow against the fresh green grass. The ploughing-up of meadows and grassland has been the main cause of the gradual decline of this lovely wild flower. However, where the slopes have been too steep to plough and cultivate, the cowslip still flourishes. You will have no difficulty in finding them in the area of Cradle Hill and Camp Hill. The word 'cowslip' is a polite name for 'cowpat', because it flowers as scattered clumps in pastures frequented by cattle. A member of the primrose family, the cowslip can be easily recognised by its crinkly leaves and long stout stalk, some 20 centimetres tall, bearing a number of small yellow drooping flowers which appear in March in a warm spring, but April and May are the months when they can be seen at their best. The root of the plant possesses many active medicinal properties. It is used in homeopathy to treat pain and breathing disorders, and in the past it was used to improve memory and cure insomnia. Young cowslip leaves were often eaten in salads. Cowslip wine can also be made from the petals, and the resultant pale yellow liquid is said to be beneficial for giddiness and nervous disorders. Truly a plant that has proved of benefit to mankind.

Violets abound in the copses and open grasslands. There are some ten species of violet growing wild in Britain, and of these three can be found in the area. One that is commonly found amongst the grass on the hillside escarpment is the *hairy violet*. About eight centimetres tall, it is easily recognised by its large, hairy, heart-shaped leaves. The flowers vary from deep blue to purple and even pure white, and are devoid of scent. Another common violet growing here is the *dog violet*, which has more or less smooth leaves and a flower spur that is paler than the petals. It can be found in the woods and copses as well as on the grassland slopes flowering in April to August, slightly later than the hairy violet.

Look out, too, for the *field pansy*, another plant of the violet family, which grows along the edges of cultivated fields. The small flowers are subject to a great variety of colour, from blue-violet to creamy white or yellow, or a combination of all of these. This plant likes chalky soils and used to be a very common species in most of our downland cornfields. As a boy I seldom walked over the hills in spring and summer without seeing masses of them. Herbicide sprays have proved their downfall, and now they can be found mainly at the edges of arable fields where the sprays have not reached.

Occasionally on the paths that cross diagonally across the escarpment, and particularly where they pass through wooded areas, you will come across patches of *deadly nightshade*. The most poisonous of our wild plants, deadly nightshade forms a bush some 120 centimetres tall, with large, egg-shaped leaves and purple drooping flowers. It blooms in June to August and forms cherry-sized globular black fruit. Although the whole plant has an unpleasant smell, the fruits, which often prove attractive to children, are particularly deadly. The juice of the fruit, under the name of atropine or belladonna, is used in modern medicine, particularly by oculists, who find it valuable for its effect when drops are put into the eye – the pupil dilates considerably, so allowing easier examination.

Not to be confused with the deadly nightshade are two common plants found flowering from June to September just about anywhere in the area, the *black nightshade* and *woody nightshade*. The berries of both plants are poisonous – the black nightshade particularly so – and they can cause severe sickness to humans if eaten. The black nightshade has small white flowers with black berries and is found growing particularly in arable fields and waste places beside paths and tracks. The woody nightshade (or *bittersweet*, as it is sometimes called) has very impressive flowers with five blue-purple petals with a central core of prominent bright yellow anthers. This plant has long trailing stems which climb up through hedges and low bushes to a height of some 100–150 centimetres. After flowering, small egg-shaped berries are formed, which go through a series of colour changes from green, through yellow and orange, to bright red. The popular name bittersweet derives from the fact that the stems, when tasted, are first bitter and then the sensation changes to one of pleasant sweetness. The stems used to be collected in autumn, then dried and used as a medicine to cure rheumatism and skin complaints.

Orchids of many kinds abound on the chalk grassland slopes. One of the most attractive and conspicuous is the *pyramidal orchid*. With its pyramid-shaped bright pink flowers and lance-shaped unspotted leaves, it often occurs in great abundance. From 20 to 60 centimetres tall, it flowers from June to August. It is a robust orchid and can quickly establish itself on new ground. In fact at Cradle Hill it was the first orchid species to establish itself in the previously cultivated area in the valley bottom. Here its flowers stand out well against the somewhat drab surroundings. A few years ago I came across a group of pure white pyramidal orchids, and how strikingly beautiful they were. This was the first time I had ever seen the white variety anywhere, and they were growing in an area where I had known the normal ones to grow every year. The white flowers have not reappeared since, so obviously they occur only intermittently. Who knows, you may be lucky and see the occasional one flowering at Cradle Hill.

In contrast to the pyramidal orchid, look very carefully in the long grass in late May or early June for the small (only six to ten centimetres high) *burnt* or *dwarf orchid*. The flowers are borne on a single stem and have a dark purple hood and a lip which is white and speckled with red. The unopened flowers at the top of the flower spike are a rich red-brown and give this orchid its name 'burnt'. This orchid is not common, and seems to be on the decline. However, it could be that because of its diminutive size it is often overlooked. It also has a tendency to disappear altogether for several years, only to reappear again in abundance. The flowers of the burnt orchid have a sweet, pleasant smell which is attractive to insects. Let us hope that these insects do their work well and this orchid continues to reproduce itself in the area.

Adding colour to the chalk slopes and pathways in June to September is the *lady's bedstraw*. The stem is some 30 centimetres long and bears whorls of some 8 to 12 slender leaves along its length. At intervals, clusters of small cruciform-shaped yellow flowers are borne on short stems. The plant forms quite large colonies in places, and these are easily seen and recognised. The flower was once used to curdle milk for the making of Cheshire cheese, and it has also been used as a dye.

Related to lady's bedstraw, but flowering somewhat earlier in May or June, is the *crosswort*. This plant grows beside the hedgerows and copses in the area and is very distinct from all the other bedstraws by having its large, egg-shaped, hairy leaves arranged crosswise in whorls of four up the stem. The yellow flowers are larger than those of the lady's bedstraw, and the plant does not form such large colonies.

Musk thistle is one of the most striking of the 13 native species of thistle in Britain, and it can be found flowering just about anywhere in the open spaces and sheltered hollows of the Downs. The erect stem can be over a metre tall, and is winged and spiny. The crimson flowers bloom from June to September and are the largest of our native thistles, some five centimetres in diameter. They hang on curved stalks in a drooping manner, giving this thistle another common name, *nodding thistle*. The flowers have an agreeable scent of musk and are visited by many bees and butter-flies.

Watch out where you sit, or you will soon find the *ground* or *stemless thistle*. This is one of the common thistles on the chalk grasslands and, as its name suggests, it has no stem and remains close to the ground, where it forms a handsome rosette of sharp, spiny leaves. The solitary crimson flower emerges from the centre of the rosette, making a quite distinctive plant. This thistle flowers from July to September. It is sometimes known as the '*picnic thistle*' because of its habit of placing itself just on the spot where you choose to sit, so giving you a sharp reminder of its presence. I cannot count the many times this has happened to me as I rested to admire the view.

You cannot miss the climbing shrub known by names such as *traveller's joy*, *wild clematis* or *old man's beard*. You will meet this at every turn around Cradle Hill as it scrambles over hedges and trees, clinging tightly by means of tough leaf stalks to any branch or shoot it touches. Its long, rope-like stems 'fling' themselves out in all directions and can grow many metres tall as they seek the light. The greenish-white, slightly scented flowers bloom from July to September. As they die they are replaced by feathery fruit, which form clusters of 'old man's beard'. When winter arrives and most of the trees and hedges are bare, the gleaming-white old man's beard give the traveller joy as he passes.

Before leaving Cradle Hill for the next area of interest, look for the dew-pond near the top of the escarpment close by the main road to Alfriston. This dew-pond is oval in shape, quite unlike most of the others, which are circular. This was probably used in ancient times to quench the thirst of horses and oxen as they toiled up the steep track which is now the main road.

I hope you have enjoyed exploring this area. Certainly in the spring and summer you will have found much of interest. Even in the middle of winter, when the earth is as hard as iron and the cold north wind sweeps down the hillsides, there is a sense of tranquillity and timelessness about the place. Here amongst the deep valleys on clear nights, uncluttered by the distant glow of street lights, you can look up and gaze at the stars and watch them as they slowly glide across the heavens. Surely this is a place where you have time to reflect on the wonderful world of nature and history, and the many people who once inhabited the area.

Cirl Bunting

8

AROUND BOSTAL HILL

Bostal Hill is the centre point of our next chapter, which includes the South Downs from Alfriston to Firle Beacon and the area either side of the magnificent north-east-facing escarpment. The whole area is steeped in history, with numerous burial mounds, dew-ponds and ancient trackways. Outstanding and picturesque views abound in all directions, from the English Channel to the south over to the green hills and forests of the High Weald in the north. The natural history in a sense is similar to that of Cradle Hill, but nevertheless certain additional habitats, such as ancient woodland and roadside edges, are worthy of note.

You can reach Bostal Hill in several ways: by road to the car park just to the west, or you can walk from Cradle Hill by way of Blackstone Bottom, as mentioned in the previous chapter. However, the most interesting route is to walk up Winton Street past the white house called The Sanctuary and then up the South Downs Way and along the escarpment ridge. Winton Street is of Neolithic origin, being the old trackway and coaching road to the strategic fording point of the Cuckmere near to Berwick Court, which existed well before Longbridge was built. On your way up the street note the very old houses to your right: Winton House, Danny Cottage, Thatchover, with its thatch sloping steeply down at the back to give protection from the cold north wind, and several others. At the top of Winton Street next to The Sanctuary is the point where five prehistoric paths met. Here, too, was a Saxon burial ground (mentioned in Chapter 1), and higher up there are tumuli and a long barrow, indicating burial places of much more ancient origin.

Stand at this place on a summer's day when white puffs of cloud are scudding across the blue sky, and look westwards over the rippling cornfields at the smooth slopes of the Downs as they sweep steeply down to the north. The view changes with the seasons, but was probably not much different in Roman times, except that then there were no church spires, no distinct system of fields, and the countryside below the Downs would have been more heavily wooded with swamp and marsh, making it impenetrable in places.

At The Sanctuary bear left up the deeply indented trackway that leads up to Long Barrow and the South Downs Way. On your right, just past The Sanctuary, there is a disused chalk pit which has much of interest in it. Search carefully amongst the chalk rubble and you may find some fossils or petrified traces of marine animals many millions of years old. The short turf around and inside this chalk pit has a wonderful variety of plants, such as *centaury, yellow-wort, horseshoe vetch, carline thistle,* and many others. See how many different species you can identify. The number will surprise you and will give you some idea of the rich rewards that await discovery as you walk up to the South Downs Way and beyond.

April and early May is the time of the year to see bird migration at its best. Sit on the side of the chalk escarpment near the top on a sunny day in April, preferably with a gentle wind from the south or south-west. You will be rewarded by the sight of *swallows* and *martins* in singles and pairs flying low and fast beneath you following the undulating slopes of the Downs. Swallows begin to arrive in late March from south of the Sahara Desert, a week or so before their close relatives the *house martin* and *sand martin.* They return slightly earlier, too, in September.

Swallows are often confused with martins, so it may be of interest to note the distinguishing features of each. The swallow has long tail feathers and a red chin with uniform blue-black upper part. Its flight is swooping, fast and graceful. The house martin has a tail which is much less deeply forked than the swallow's, and it also has white underparts with a distinct white rump near the tail. Its flight is less swooping and more fluttering than the swallow. The sand martin, the smallest of the three, has earthy-brown upper parts and white underparts with a broad brown band across its chest.

The swallow constructs a cup-shaped nest of mud, straw and grass, lined with feathers, on top of rafters in outbuildings such as old barns. The house martin, on the other hand, builds its dome-shaped nest of mud, lined with bits of grass and feathers, close up under the eaves of homes or under bridges. It has an elliptical entrance hole at the top, directly under the eave of the house. The sand martin, as its name might suggest, nests in steep sandy banks along rivers or in quarries. It constructs a tunnel into the bank some half to one metre in depth, at the end of which is a small chamber lined with loose vegetable matter and feathers which are gathered in flight. All three species return to the same nesting site year after year, and both the martins nest in quite large colonies of up to 30 or 40 pairs. Also all three each lay from four to six white eggs (speckled with red in the case of the swallow) from May to July.

House martins and swallows could certainly nest just about anywhere in this area, but it is doubtful if there is now a colony of sand martins here. I well remember as a boy spending hours watching sand martins in a colony just behind Selmeston Church in a very ancient sandpit. What a delight they were as they flitted around the hedgerows and trees, catching insects on the wing to feed to their young. They made little sound except a weak twittering, hardly audible against the rustle of leaves in the wind. Sadly, this colony gradually declined as the years passed, and was deserted altogether in the 1960s.

The *swift* is not of the same tribe as the swallows and martins; nevertheless, it is a bird that you will see with the others on this migration route along the South Downs. The swift can be distinguished at a glance from swallows and martins by its very long, scythe-shaped wings and by its overall sooty-black plumage. Like the house martin and swallow, it relies on man's activities to provide a nesting site. It constructs a nest of aerially collected material, such as grass and feathers, in holes and crevices of large houses or church towers. The two white eggs are laid in May or June, and only one brood per year is produced. The young swifts grow slowly and spend much longer than most birds in the nest, some six weeks in all. This fact may explain why the swift begins its migration back to South Africa early in August, a good month or so before many other species. Swallows and martins often rear a second brood, and this of course delays their departure until late in September or October. The swift, on the other hand, with the long fledgling period of its young, has little time to rear a second brood, and thus has no reason to delay the start of its long southward flight.

Swifts are prodigious fliers; not only is their flight fast and strong, but they remain in the air most of their lives. Because of the swift's short, feeble legs and long wings, it has great difficulty in rising from level ground, and therefore only alights by accident. At one time it was thought that after dark, when incubating eggs, both birds were at the nest together. However, it is now known that the bird which is not incubating or brooding young stays aloft in the air until sunrise. The birds feed, mate and even sleep while soaring and gliding high up in the sky on currents of air. The swift can rightly be considered as one of our more remarkable and interesting birds.

Although there is some mystery about the reason why birds migrate northwards in spring to our shores from far-off Africa, there is nothing unusual about the southwards migration in autumn of birds such as *fieldfares* and *redwings* from their breeding grounds in the forests of Scandinavia. They come here to escape the cold, harsh northern winters and to find food. The redwing can be recognised by its eye-stripe, reddish flanks and, when in flight, the chestnut colouring under its wings. The fieldfare is larger, has a grey head and rump, and a rusty-coloured back. Both these birds arrive in late September and can be seen throughout the winter in groups in the large fields above and below the Downs, seeking food, mainly insects and worms, amongst the stubble and vegetable remains. Both redwings and fieldfares can be found in mixed groups while feeding, and often one bird acts as lookout, sitting as high as possible on a post, bush or tree. Try to spot this bird with binoculars before it gives a harsh chattering alarm call which sets the birds to flight. Redwings begin to leave for the north again in late March, slightly before the fieldfare, but both have gone by May.

The buzzard is a bird of prey that is commonly associated with the West Country and Scotland, where it breeds regularly. In the early nineteenth century the *common buzzard*, as it is known, was widespread throughout England, Wales and Scotland. However, its main food source is the *rabbit*, which was also valued by man for its meat. So the buzzard was persecuted and killed in large numbers, and its decline throughout the nineteenth and early twentieth centuries was aided by the spread of industrialisation and the reclamation of waste lands. After the First World War the numbers of buzzards began to increase as the rabbit population exploded. By 1952 the buzzard had spread back south and south-east into Dorset, Hampshire and Sussex. But the introduction of myxomatosis into the rabbit population between 1952 and 1955, leading to its virtual extinction, was bad luck for the buzzard, which then went back into decline. In recent years the number of rabbits rapidly increased as they became resistant to myxomatosis, and the buzzard is back with us in Sussex. A pair now breeds somewhere in the area, and I have occasionally watched one soaring and flying in slow wide circles over the woodlands beneath Bostal Hill as it searches for rabbits and rodents.

The common buzzard has dark brown plumage with narrow dark bars on its tail. In flight, buzzards can be distinguished by their broad wings and large rounded tails. Within its own territories, a buzzard has its favourite hunting perch on which it sits watching for prey. When it sees something, it moves its head from side to side, pinpointing the exact spot, then descends in a gentle glide and finally pounces. The buzzard also hovers like a kestrel, and when its prey is sighted it drops silently by partly closing its wings until, when just above the ground, it plunges rapidly onto its target. About ten unsuccessful attacks are made for each one that succeeds. After a kill the buzzard, unlike the kestrel, does not usually rise immediately but can be seen pecking at the prey caught in its talons. Large prey such as rabbits are taken to a perch for dismembering; smaller ones are eaten whole.

The buzzard builds a substantial structure of branches as a nest and lines it with vegetable material such as bracken, moss and green leaves. The finished structure is some 60 centimetres across and is placed either on a cliff ledge or in the fork of a tree. In the case of the pair around Bostal Hill, the nest is almost certainly in a tree in one of the woods at the foot of the Downs. The two or three eggs are usually laid in April, and the young hatch out after about 37 days in late May. This coincides with the emergence of many young rabbits, which are caught by both parents and fed to their fledglings. The young buzzards receive food from their parents for another month or so before they finally leave the nest to fend for themselves. With the present increasing rabbit population, evident to all who observe the countryside, it must be hoped that our pair of resident buzzards will be successful and that this magnificent bird will survive and multiply.

Another bird one might expect to see in this locality is the *corn bunting*. Much larger than that other bunting, the yellowhammer, mentioned in the previous chapter, the corn bunting is a dull-coloured, heavily built bird that may be seen perched conspicuously on a fence post bordering the cultivated fields at the top of the escarpment. It has a distinctive rapid song which sounds like 'the jangling of a bunch of keys'. In recent years the corn bunting has been scarce on the Sussex Downs, but as I write their numbers have increased, and you should have little difficulty in spotting one. The male bird has an extraordinary polygamous habit, and may have up to seven hen birds as mates. No wonder he takes little part in nest-building, incubation or feeding young, as he is always kept busy watching over his family and defending his territory against other males. The female bird builds her nest of grass, roots and leaves about a metre off the ground, in the base of a hedgerow or shrub. The three to five eggs are laid in June or July, which is late compared with most of our breeding birds. The eggs hatch quickly after only about 12 or 13 days, and the young are in the nest for only about 10 days before they fly. The corn bunting often produces two broods, and cases of three broods have been recorded. Corn buntings eat seeds, caterpillars, ants and any other small vegetable or animal matter they can find. In winter they are often seen in small flocks mingling with larger flocks of sparrows and yellowhammers as they search for food.

You may be lucky enough to see that beautiful bird the *cirl bunting*. The male has yellow underparts, yellow and black head, and black throat. The female is much duller and is similar to a female yellowhammer, but has an olive-brown rump. Cirl buntings are a Mediterranean species and are rare in this country. It is unlikely that they nest in this area. However, a few years ago in April I watched a pair for several hours as they moved along the hedges and in the fields around Bopeep Farm. It could well be that the warmer climate of the last few years will persuade this lovely bird to settle and breed under the Downs.

The wonderful grassy slopes of the escarpment are a haven for the skylark and meadow pipit. The *skylark* is a bird of the wide open spaces, and it avoids trees and hedges of any kind. On the ground it is inconspicuous with its dull brown plumage and short, rounded crest. However, when the skylark is in the air it is easily recognised as it hangs on fluttering wings and pours out its liquid song. This song, which is most often heard from March to July, is very long and sustained, and is delivered usually while the bird hovers in flight or is gently descending to the ground. Sometimes the bird sings on the ground or from a low perch. The skylark builds its nest of grass on the ground. The three to five dark brown speckled eggs are laid from April to July, and two broods are common. The incubating female sits quite tightly on the nest, so if a skylark flies up suddenly from close to your feet, stop and look very carefully in the grass around you. Take great care not to tread on the nest and its contents. The skylark is basically a ground-living bird that feeds on seeds and insects, and because of this and its nesting habits, it is vulnerable to over-grazing by cattle and by intensive farming where meadows and crops are sprayed and cut by machine. Skylark numbers on the South Downs have declined in recent years, but from my own observations skylarks have returned in fair numbers to areas of land which have been allowed to return to nature under the set-aside scheme. We must do all that we can to ensure that the lark's song is forever heard in the clear air on the Downs and fields of our countryside.

More numerous than the skylark on the downland slopes is the *meadow pipit*. This brown, rather nondescript bird is often seen flitting across the grass calling 'pheet-pheet-pheet' in a shrill voice. In summer it performs a short territorial song-flight which ends in a 'parachute descent'. Like the skylark, it builds its nest on the ground in a tussock of grass. The eggs are similar to those of the skylark, but smaller. The young of both species grow fast, and when they leave the nest they quickly learn to freeze when danger approaches, relying on their natural camouflage for protection.

Both the skylark and meadow pipit congregate in quite large flocks to feed, especially in winter, when they are joined by those that nested in the north and are retreating southwards from approaching cold weather.

Many of the butterflies mentioned in the previous chapter can be seen around Bostal Hill, including *chalkhill blues, meadow browns* and *marbled whites.*

A blue butterfly species not yet mentioned is the *brown argus.* As its name implies, it is not blue in colour but both sexes are dark brown with a black spot in the centre of the their fore-wings. Both sexes too have orange 'half-moons' around the edge of their wings. The male is slightly smaller and more brightly coloured than the female. Look out for these gregarious butterflies on a sunny day in June or July. They like to be together in small groups as they flit between the many kinds of wild flowers on which they feed. The brown argus is confined to the south of England and the north and south coasts of Wales, where the two food plants of its caterpillar can be found, the *common rockrose* on the chalk downs and the *storksbill* along the coasts. The common rockrose is found fairly frequently on this part of the Downs and is a very dwarf shrub with short prostrate stems and small shiny leaves that grow in pairs. The underside of the leaves is whitish and downy. The comparatively large flowers are pale yellow and bloom from June to September. The brown argus lays its eggs singly on the underside of the leaves of the rockrose. The adult butterflies emerge from the chrysalids in April to August, and each lives for only two or three weeks. I hope you will see this butterfly; by experience and with the help of a specialist butterfly book you will learn to distinguish it from the similar-looking females of other blue species.

From the car park near Bostal Hill, walk down the road that leads to the main A27 Lewes to Polegate road. It is a walk full of interest and fine views. At the beginning the lane carves its way through the chalk slopes, and on either side from early spring to late autumn can be seen many different wild flowers, including several species of orchids. One particular plant that will strike you as out of place is the *wild pink*, which forms a large patch on the steep eastern slope. It flowers from June to August and brings a lovely touch of colour, adding to those from its many companions. This particular plant was probably a garden escape, but it has been recorded as growing here as long ago as 1935. Lower down, the road passes across cultivated fields of corn and then through the edge of an ancient woodland, Tilton Wood. This wood is private property, but much of interest can be discovered near the roadside edges.

On your way down the lane, look out for patches of *honey-suckle*, for at dusk on a summer's day you may be fortunate enough to spot a *convolvulus hawk-moth* with its long proboscis, feeding on the nectar of this plant. This moth, with its wingspan of 12 centimetres, is the largest of any British insect. It is grey in colour and has a stout body banded in pink and white. Like most moths, the convolvulus hawk-moth is nocturnal, and by day it rests on tree trunks and posts, where its colour makes it difficult to be seen. Like many of the hawk-moths, it seldom breeds in Britain because it is too cold, and it arrives here as a migrant from the Mediterranean in early summer. A powerful flier, it can travel 1,000 kilometres or so in just a few days.

Just occasionally you may see something that looks like a small humming-bird hovering with fast-beating wings in front of a honeysuckle or periwinkle flower. This is the *hummingbird hawk-moth*, which is another migrant from southern Europe and the Mediterranean. A grey moth with orange hind wings, it is quite small, with a wingspan of only about six centimetres. It is uncommon, but in some years huge numbers arrive mostly in southern England, and a few will breed, laying their eggs on one of the species of bedstraw plants. Unlike the convolvulus hawk-moth, this species is a day flier and can be found at just about any time on hot summer days between June and September. It has a characteristic darting action, and often disappears quickly, only to reappear a few seconds later.

A butterfly you will almost certainly see in the area of Tilton Wood on a warm spring day in April or May is the *orange tip*. One of the five white species of butterfly, the orange tip is so called because the male has bright orange wing-tips, while those of the female are black. The male is very distinctive as it flies along the roadside ditches and damp areas amongst woods where its favourite food plants grow, such as *Jack-by-the-hedge*, *lady's smock* and many others of the cabbage family. This butterfly very seldom alights with open wings, because with its dappled green and white undersides it can remain well disguised amongst the flowers. While the male patrols his territory, the female flies in search of food plants on which to lay her eggs. These small eggs are laid amongst flower heads, typically in lady's smock, and are greenish-white at first, changing in the later stages to orange. The bluish-green caterpillars hatch out after about 25 days. They feed on the flowers, buds and leaves of the food plant, and are known to be cannibalistic, eating any smaller orange tip caterpillar they encounter. The caterpillars have long forked hairs which secrete a sweet liquid upon which ants feed. Only one generation a year is produced, and the adult butterflies only live for about 18 days.

What a variety of wild flowers are to be found here. The escarpment slopes have many of the chalk downland flowers mentioned in earlier chapters, and the small copses and woods lower down contain many ancient woodland species. In 1952 I was cycling along the A27 near Selmeston when a large white flower spike at the base of roadside bushes caught my eye. I stopped to investigate and was excited to make my first discovery of the *greater butterfly orchid*. Further searches of the local area revealed other patches of this uncommon plant. The stem is 20 to 60 centimetres high and bears 10 to 25 large white flowers, each with a long strap-shaped labellum pointing downwards and a long spur containing nectar. The flowers have a strong, sweet smell which intensifies at night to attract night-flying moths. At the base of the stem are two large pale green oval leaves, above which are several small pointed stem leaves. The butterfly orchid seems to favour shady spots in woods below the Downs where the soil is heavy and moss-covered. It flourishes particularly well beside woodland streams where the soil is moist. The flowers appear in late May and throughout June. Sadly, the site I knew at Selmeston has long since been destroyed by road widening, but

I hope you still find this beautiful and exotic orchid flowering beside woods nearby.

Along the roadside near Tilton Wood you will notice a tall greenish plant with two large oval leaves at its base. This is the *common twayblade orchid.* Insignificant and dull it might look, but when carefully examined it is an interesting orchid with a charm all its own. The twayblade flowers from April to July, the 20 to 40 yellowish-green flowers being borne on a stout stem densely covered with downy hairs. It is widely distributed in Britain and grows in many habitats, ranging from damp woods to dry chalk downs. The plant varies in height from 20 to 75 centimetres, those growing in shady woods being taller than those growing on the open downland. Look closely at the flowers and you will see that the lip or labellum divides into two lobes. At the base of the labellum you will notice a groove down which honey is secreted. The flower is fertilised by small beetles and flies which visit to lick up the honey from the groove. In crawling up the groove the insect's head is instantly smeared with a sticky glue and pollen. It takes fright and goes off to another flower, fully laden with pollen in the right place for effective fertilisation. Many a small beetle or fly may be seen about the twayblades with their heads bearing a bunch of pollinia which they have gathered from the flowers. A high proportion of the flowers produce ripe seed capsules, but the seeds take about four years to develop into the characteristic two-leaved plant, and it is a further ten years before it flowers. So you may find many plants with just two large leaves and no stem. The common twayblade can also reproduce itself vegetatively by developing buds on its fleshy, fibrous roots, which shoot off in all directions around the parent plant. This method often takes place in woods where it is too dark for flowers to bloom.

Before leaving the area of Tilton Wood, look out for the lovely yellow flowers of the *evening primrose.* This is not a natural species, but was introduced as a garden plant from North America and has now spread throughout the country, growing in waste places. Look for it in the summer months at the side of the lane where it joins the A27. A robust and hairy plant, it is about a metre tall, with leafy stems and large oblong leaves which form a rosette at the base. The quite large yellow flowers are made up of four petals and are about five centimetres across. The flowers open towards the evening and are pollinated by night-flying moths. In 1949 it was discovered that the clear, pale yellow oil that came out of the seeds of this plant was rich in the fatty acids essential for the well-being of the human body. This evening primrose oil is now used widely to treat patients suffering from nervous disorders such as multiple sclerosis.

A profusion of orchids is to be found on the slopes just to the east of Firle Beacon. Here, look for the fragrant and common spotted orchids. The *fragrant orchid* varies from about 15 to 60 centimetres tall, the single stem carrying up to 200 rosy-purple flowers in a fairly dense spike. The flowers are strongly sweet-scented, hence its name, and bloom in June and July. At the base of the plant are three to five long narrow leaves, while the stem carries another two or three leaves whose lower parts are wrapped closely around it. All the leaves are without spots. You may be fortunate enough to discover, amongst the hundreds that adorn these slopes, the pure white form of the fragrant orchid. Flowering at the same time and in the same places is the *common spotted orchid.* This is easily distinguished from the fragrant orchid by its pale lilac flowers, which are only faintly scented, and by its leaves, which in nearly all cases are covered in brownish-purple blotches.

One of my earliest memories of orchids is walking near Firle Beacon one autumn day and finding a short stem densely covered in white hairs and bearing numerous small white flowers arranged in a very distinct spiral. On returning home to my books I easily identified my find as *autumn lady's-tresses.* This lovely little orchid flowers in August and September, and is a plant of dry calcareous soils where the turf is short. The flower stem is only 5 to 15 centimetres tall, and at first sight it appears to have no leaves. However, a closer inspection of the base of the stem reveals the withered remains of the leaves amongst the grass. Close by the stem and to one side you will find, in September, two or three very fresh bluish-green leaves which are still developing. These persist over winter and from their centre will grow next year's flowering stem. In some years autumn lady's-tresses flower in great numbers, and in other years they are infrequent or entirely absent. In the nearby village of East Dean this orchid flourishes on lawns which are made up of the original downland turf, and in some years many thousands appear, particularly if the lawn is left uncut. In other years, hardly any can be seen. The reasons for these fluctuations are not fully understood, but weather and mycorrhizal activity are certainly factors. From my limited obser-vations, a wet spring seems to lead to a profusion of orchid flowers in late August.

If you look carefully amongst the close-cropped turf on these slopes, you will come across a very low herb whose bright flowers seem to peep out from the grasses throughout the summer. This is the *eyebright*, which grows to a height of only about five centimetres on the Downs. It has deeply cut dark green oval leaves which grow in pairs up the central stem. You will see how attractive the flowers are if you examine them with a hand lens. White, with beautiful markings of purple and yellow, they bloom from May to September, and are borne near the extremities of the branches. There are many different varieties of eyebright, and their Latin name is derived from a Greek word '*euphraisio*', meaning to delight or gladden, an allusion to the pleasing colours of their flowers or to the joy of having eye complaints cured with their extracts. In medieval times eyebright potions supposedly cured dimness of vision and short-sightedness. Herbalists also prepared a powder from this plant which was used for brightening the eyes. Nicholas Culpeper, a seventeenth-century astrologer-physician, writes of eyebright: 'If the herb was as much used as it is neglected, it would half spoil the spectacle-maker's trade; and a man would prefer that reason should teach people to prefer the preservation of their natural before artificial spectacles.' That lovely bird the *linnet* is fond of pecking at eyebright, but I don't know how to recognise a short-sighted linnet! The eyebright is part parasite, in that it attaches its roots to other plants, particularly grasses, and robs them of sustenance. However, interestingly enough, if its seeds are sown in a pot they easily germinate and grow, but never into large, robust plants.

Growing amongst the orchids and eyebrights is the *round-headed rampion*. A plant of the chalk downs of southern England, the round-headed rampion is commonest in Sussex, and is also known as '*the pride of Sussex*'. About 30 to 50 centimetres tall, it has at its base a number of long-stalked lance-shaped leaves with rounded teeth. The few stem-leaves are stalkless. The small dark blue flowers are closely clustered and form globe-shaped heads some two to three centimetres in diameter at the end of the long stems. They flower in July and August and make a marvellous sight as they sway back and forth in the wind. If you are lucky you may see one visited by a burnet moth, and the contrasting colours of black, blue and red are pleasing to the eye.

We often take a gentle breeze for granted, and never consider how it affects and enhances the beauty of our surroundings. How often have I thrown myself down on my back here amongst the dry, crisp grasses and colourful flowers of the South Downs and looked up at the blue depths of the sky. I feel in a different world as I watch the cottony clouds creep slowly to the horizon and think about the stars that I know to be there although hidden by the bright light of the sun. How splendid it would be if I could reach up, catch them in my hand and see what they are about. But let them be as Longfellow wrote in *Evangeline*:

> Silently one by one in the infinite meadows of heaven
> Blossomed the lovely stars, the forget-me-nots of the angels.

I turn my head sideways and see the play of the wind as it ripples through the grasses and sways the flowers with their multitude of colours. Looking to the horizon, I see the cloud shadows sliding with the wind across the hills and woods, and patches of sunlight that suddenly appear bringing bright colours to the cultivated fields and hedgerows. I fall into timeless contemplation and wonder what all this was like five hundred, a thousand or five thousand years ago. Who was here and how did they live? I would love to go back in time just to see, but I must be able to return quickly to the present. I awake from my reverie and return to the plants I love.

A common and characteristic weed growing on the downland slopes is *yellow rattle*. It is a semi-parasite, its roots drawing food from neighbouring grasses and herbs. Growing up to 40 centimetres tall, it has coarsely toothed leaves, and its straight stem terminates in a cluster of yellow flowers which bloom from May until August. Each flower has an upper hood and a lower lip, and after flowering it develops into a swollen, bladder-like capsule which contains numerous seeds. When the plant is shaken, these seeds make a distinct rattling sound, hence the flower's name.

From July to September you may come across one of the gentian family of flowers, *felwort*. About 5 to 15 centimetres tall, the felwort (or *autumn gentian*, as it is sometimes called) grows in dry pastures on the Downs. The leaves at the base are spoon-shaped, while the paired stem-leaves are lance-shaped. The five-petalled pale purple flowers are borne on stems branching out from the top of the main stem. Occasionally you will find plants which bear both four and five-petalled flowers.

Growing in similar places and at the same time as felwort is the *yellow-wort*. Another flower of the gentian family, it is easily distinguished by its eight-petalled bright yellow flowers, which are borne at the end of branched stems. Yellow-wort grows some 10 to 30 centimetres high, and is smooth overall with a peculiar glaucous hue. The base leaves are spoon-shaped and form a rosette around the erect stem. The stem-leaves are in pairs and are fused together in such a way as to make a complete collar round the stem. These leaves make it difficult for crawling insects to climb up the smooth stems to the flowers, leaving pollination to be effected by those that can fly.

As I mentioned at the beginning of this chapter, the area around Bostal Hill is full of interest, and it is important, too, for the great variety of plants that grow there. Having walked there, you must have been impressed by the all-round scenic views from on top of the escarpment. To the north spread out beneath you like a patchwork quilt is an area containing much of interest. With binoculars you can view church spires, country houses and the green domes of the now redundant observatory at Herstmonceux. You will also see the warm red tiles on top of Sussex flintstone cottages contrasting with ugly modern barns made of grey corrugated metals; and close by, just below you, as William Wordsworth so eloquently describes them, 'These hedgerows, hardly hedgerows, little lines of sportive wood run wild'. The countryside is all before you, ever changing with the seasons, and yet, within it, nature itself has not changed much over time. True, modern transport has brought more noise and some pollution, but tranquil areas still abound. All this could change if the proposal to build a modern town upon the green fields and wide open spaces of this pleasant land is revived. Do we really need to construct a town in such a place? For this would destroy what nature has sustained for so long. Certainly if this were to come about we would lose a quality of life, a tranquillity and a resource that would never return. The Downs, too, being so close by, would become overcrowded, losing their uniqueness, peace and beauty.

Common Snipe

9

BURLOW CASTLE TO FARNESTREET

Where and what, you may ask, is Burlow Castle? Burlow Castle, or what remains of it, is situated on a chalk bluff of the Downs about one kilometre north-east of Longbridge, near Alfriston. It is marked 'Burlough Castle' on Ordnance Survey maps, but spelt 'Burlow' on the oldest known reference to it, a drawing of the castle ruins made in 1770 and now kept in the British Museum. 'Burlow' is a Saxon word meaning 'a defended place', and certainly anyone visiting the site of this castle would agree that it is worthy of that name. It overlooks the very ancient fording place of the Cuckmere River, just below Berwick Court, where a gravel outcrop made the river shallow. This was the main river crossing well before Longbridge itself was built, probably in Saxon times. As such, it was a very strategic position, to be defended at all costs by any group of people who wished to dominate and control the area.

The origin of Burlow Castle is steeped in mystery and legend. Many dispute the fact that a castle existed on the site at all, and point to early fifteenth-century documents that mention a Middleton Castle existing on a site a short distance to the south at a place called 'The Rookery'. This place is a mound, probably of Norman origin, which was possibly used as a fortification. The word 'rookery' only describes trees and a place where a colony of *rooks* has established itself, and, of course, these birds were a source of food in olden days. The rook colony existed in elm trees in the early 1960s, but then Dutch elm disease destroyed the trees and the rooks moved elsewhere. Originally the Cuckmere River flowed beside The Rookery and under the bastion of Burlow Castle, and its course can still be clearly seen today as a water-filled ditch. Could The Rookery have been a site which troops used as a small harbour to go to and from the castle itself? It is known that even in recent history quite large vessels did indeed sail up and down the river.

I have examined the site of Burlow Castle with its present owner and have been shown many of the artefacts found there: stone axes, pottery, coins, a cup pebble and many pieces of bricks and ancient mortar. Most significant to my mind are the many pieces of mortar that badgers are continually digging out from their setts. Many large pieces of dressed stone are also still on the site, and it is known that the two barns of nearby Milton Court were built in the 1830s using flints from the castle ruins.

Evidence that the site was one of some importance can be presumed from the names of some places close by. For instance, Butt Lane, just to the east, indicates its ancient use by archers, and a field next to the castle has always been known as the Running Field, i.e. a field where fighting men could exercise. Interestingly, a large field just below Burlow Castle is known as Mag Mere, and is reported to be the last known home of the fairies in Sussex, Queen Mag being the mythical Queen of the Fairies!

Whatever its origins, the site of Burlow Castle, which is private property, is a grand place for natural history. The steep wooded river cliff, which protected the castle from the west and is 20 metres high, is the home of *kestrels, sparrowhawks, foxes, badgers* and *dormice*. Below it in the wetlands are *marsh orchids, marsh marigold, snipe* and *redshank* to name but a few of the interesting species of plants and birds.

Our exploration starts at the public footpath that leads northwards from Milton Street and passes just below and to the east of the castle. This sunken trackway could well have been a defensive ditch, protecting it on its most vulnerable side from the higher ground that rises up to Windover Hill. The hedgerow on the eastern side of the footpath is estimated to be 1,000 years old. It is easy to make such an estimate by counting the number of different shrubs and trees which grow in a 25-metre stretch. Each different type accounts for approximately 100 years of age. I counted several sections of this hedge, and consistently there were about 10 or 11 species, made up mainly of *wayfaring tree, hawthorn, dog rose, ash, field maple, dogwood, sycamore, buckthorn, rowan, privet* and *elm*.

As you walk up this ancient trackway, look out for the *false-brome grass* growing on the banks. One of the 150 or more species of grasses to be found in Britain, the false-brome is a tall grass, up to a metre high, with soft light green leaves. The long green flowers appear from July to September and form loose spikes at the end of the main stem.

The *sweet violet*, too, can be found growing in quantities along the bank, where it is truly a wild plant and not a garden escape. It is easily distinguished from the many other species of violet by the sweet scent of its purple, blue or white flowers and by its long runners. The runners are tough thongs which grow several centimetres long then take root and grow into another plant. The sweet violet also reproduces itself by forming seeds in the normal course of pollination by insects. The flowers are one of our earliest to bloom and can be found any month from February onwards until early summer. The large heart-shaped leaves are glossy when they just unfurl, but as they expand they take on a somewhat downy appearance. On a day towards the end of winter when the sun's warmth begins to be felt on the grassy banks, there is excitement and fulfilled expectancy in finding this plant in bloom as it heralds the approach of spring and the awakening of nature in all its wonder and splendour.

As the path approaches the main A27 road, on your right you will see a small pond surrounded by reeds, including the *reedmace* and interesting plants such as brooklime and creeping cinquefoil. *Brooklime* has a creeping stem which is thick and succulent and roots itself in the mud of the streams and watery places where it grows. The leaves are oval, smooth and grow in pairs along the stem. They used to be eaten in salads and were supposed to be a cure for scurvy. The very pretty blue flowers appear in May and continue throughout the summer. The *creeping cinquefoil* is a common plant in southern England and it seems to have been well established in this place for many years. Creeping cinquefoil is another plant that reproduces itself by runners which root themselves in the ground. It is easily identified by its five-petalled bright yellow flowers, which bloom from June to September. It has astrigent properties and was used as a cure for fever by ancient man.

You may disturb a *snipe* feeding amongst the reeds and probing the mud with its long bill for worms. You will recognise it instantly as it flies off the ground at surprising speed in a zigzag flight, calling 'scape-scape'. The snipe used to be a fairly common nesting bird in the water-meadows and marshes along the Cuckmere Valley. As a boy I found many of their nests, which were just hollows in tussocks of reed, lined with grass. The four pear-shaped olive-green eggs, spotted and blotched with brown, are laid in April to June. Sadly, I doubt if the snipe nests in this area now, as some of the meadows have been drained and human disturbance has increased greatly. However, you may still be lucky enough to hear the snipe marking out its territory in spring with a peculiar display flight. It flies high, and every now and again it dives, and the wind vibrating through its feathers makes a distinct 'drumming' noise. The bird repeats this drumming flight many times as it circles its territory.

When the first rains occur in autumn and the ground is still warm, hundreds of *field mushrooms* appear as if by magic in the fields near the pond. You can distinguish a mushroom from other fungi mainly by its white cap and dark purplish-brown gills, which are first white and then pink in the first few days of growth. Be careful to make a correct identification before eating them, and do not rely on such incorrect remarks as 'if they peel easily they are edible'.

Crossing the A27, the path continues across cultivated fields of wheat and the old pre-war Wilmington airfield just above Sherman Bridge. As you walk long the path the views to Firle Beacon and Mount Caburn are outstanding, and just about any time in spring and summer you will hear the skylark singing in the air high above you. You may also see a buzzard as it slowly circles in graceful flight looking for rabbits in the distant fields. In the autumn large flocks of lapwings fly busily around as they search for food. This high spot is a pleasant place at any time of the year, but linger not, as even more delights await you as you descend into the valley just to the south of the railway line.

In this valley bottom, to the east of the path is a large area of wetland composed largely of *common reed grass*, a lovely tall willowy grass with rough leaves that cut like a razor and feathery flower spikes of light purple that turn to a brownish-white in autumn. Stop and listen to the soft rustling of its leaves in the wind. At this same place in the spring the harsh 'churring' of the *sedge warbler* can be heard as it flits to and fro through the reeds and swampy thickets.

The sedge warbler is a small sprightly bird with brown plumage and a distinct light eye-stripe. Another migrant from Africa, it arrives in April, about a week or so before its close relative, the *reed warbler*, which can be distinguished by its absence of a prominent eye-stripe and its more musical song. The sedge warbler builds its deep, cup-shaped nest of grass and moss, lined with horse hairs low down in thick vegetation of sedges, grass, reeds or rushes. The five or six pale yellowish eggs, mottled with brown, are laid in May and June. In June or July, if you are patient and prepared to lie still on the bank above the reed-bed, you may see the parent birds flying around catching insects and grubs for their newly hatched young.

The River Cuckmere is close by; take a walk to its banks and you are almost certain to come across a pair of *mute swans*, which for many years have nested close by. The nest, a huge mound of locally collected vegetable material, must be the most prominent and visible of all British nests. The three to twelve pale green eggs are laid in late March to May. Both parents take turn about in sitting on the nest and incubating the eggs. The one on sentry duty nearby will attack fiercely any living thing, including humans, which get near to the nest. Many times I have encountered the menacing angry hisses of this large bird and have never been able to photograph its eggs. The mute swan was first introduced into this country from Cyprus by Richard I in about 1189. Mute swans are protected birds and those not marked as belonging to specific ownership belong to the Queen.

Anywhere along the side of the river or amongst the sedges and rushes that grow nearby you are likely to put up a *moorhen* which rises from the water with a pattering of feet along the surface and uttering a harsh penetrating 'kittok'. A common bird to be found on most ponds and areas of water, the moorhen is distinguished by its dark plumage, red forehead and white stripe along its flank. It generally builds its nest of reeds, rushes and grass on the ground, amongst the water plants that grow beside the river. The seven to twelve buff-coloured eggs, spotted and speckled with reddish-brown, are laid from March to as late as August. The eggs hatch after three weeks and the young leave the nest as little bundles of black 'fur' in two or three days. The moorhen feeds on just about anything it can find, from slugs and worms to insects, seeds and waterweed, and it frequently devours the eggshells after the eggs have hatched, to retain the necessary calcium and mineral salts in its body. A poor flier, the moorhen is truly at home in the water, where it spends the whole year near thick undergrowth in which it can hide if danger threatens. It can even remain submerged for quite long periods with just its bill above water. It is a very aggressive bird, and I have heard reports of it attacking other small ducklings by sitting on top of them in the water.

Amongst the marshy places and reed-beds you will almost certainly come across the *reed bunting*. The male is very conspic-uous with its black head and throat and white collar, but the female is duller and lacks these distinguishing features. You will often see the reed bunting singing from on top of a reed-stem or bush. The song begins slowly 'tseek, tseek, tseek' and ends in a hurried 'tssissisk'. In the spring, when nest-building commences, it is fairly easy to watch the birds back to the site of their nest. The nest, which is made of dried grasses lined with hair, is built low down in tussocks of reeds or sedges. The four to seven purplish-grey eggs, spotted with dark purple, are laid from March to July. When disturbed off their nest, either parent will often feign a broken wing and shuffle across the ground trying to lead the intruder away from the nest. This ruse is attempted particularly when there are young in the nest.

The river here, just below the railway bridge, is a restful place at any time of the year, but come here in August and see some of its aquatic plants. The *great hairy willowherb*, a metre or so tall, with its large four-petalled rose-coloured flowers and hairy lance-shaped leaves, grows prolifically beside the water's edge. Its country name, *codlins-and-cream*, is derived from the odour of the flowers, 'codlin' being a type of apple. In early autumn you can see the white feathery seeds of the great hairy willowherb flying haphazardly across the water with the wind.

You may come across one of the prettiest hawk-moths in Britain here, the *elephant hawk-moth*. With a wingspan of seven centimetres, this delicately pink hawk-moth is a night flier, but may be seen on June evenings just about anywhere where willowherbs grow. Although feeding on the nectar of such flowers as honeysuckle and bramble, this moth lays its eggs on willowherb species. The caterpillar is browny-grey with two huge eye-spots, and defends itself by extending its head and neck like an elephant's trunk. This gives the caterpillar a menacing and frightening appearance. You are quite likely to see this caterpillar more often than the moth. Look for it on willowherb leaves at any time in July or August.

The *purple loosestrife* is another handsome wild flower that grows here beside the river. About a metre tall, it has long narrow spikes of starry-shaped reddish-purple flowers and narrow hairy leaves. It flowers in August and September. In similar places, look out for the *marsh woundwort*, with its short hollow stems, narrow leaves and pale reddish-purple flowers grouped in whorls of six or more at intervals along the upper part of the stem. It also flowers in August and September. The *water pepper* grows on wet, muddy banks, an erect, slender yellowish-green plant with long spikes of well-separated flowers which often droop at the tip. The lance-shaped green leaves are downy underneath and have a peppery taste. The leaves also contain an acrid juice which can irritate the skin on top of the hand and between the fingers.

You cannot fail to see the beautiful large yellow flowers of the *yellow water lily*, with its thick leathery heart-shaped leaves floating on the surface. Watch them as they are blown upright by the wind as it ripples across the water. This water lily is also known as *brandy bottle* on account of its fruit, which ripens on the water's surface in the shape of a flagon.

What a wonderful place to be in high summer. The mute swan glides past, looking with suspicion and a slight hint of menace as it leads four cygnets in trail behind it. A distant skylark sings high in the air and a flock of goldfinches twitter on the breeze as they seek out thistle heads for food. Suddenly you hear a movement in the water, and see a *water vole* scramble to cover in the bank.

Returning to the path just before it crosses the railway line, there is a patch of lower greensand, the name given to a sand that contains green particles of iron minerals. This outcrop of greensand has its own particular flora and insect population. One common plant to be found here is the *sheep's sorrel*. This plant is a relative of the dock family and is fairly small, usually only about 15 centimetres tall. The arrow-shaped leaves form a thick rosette at the base of the plant. The small green drooping flowers, tinged with red, appear from May to August and the whole plant is made conspicuous in the latter half of the year by its foliage developing a bright red tint. The leaves are often used to add an agreeable pungency to salads.

A butterfly that lays its eggs on the upper surfaces of the sorrel plant is the *small copper*. This is a beautiful bright butterfly with copper-coloured wings and is often seen basking with wings open on flowers. It is quick to fly off and intercept other butterflies that may intrude onto its territory. Two generations are produced each year, and they are seen on the wing from April to October. The caterpillars feed on sorrel plants and are well camouflaged, the early ones being green and the later ones being green-pink to match the change in colour of the host plant.

Another butterfly to be found on this sandy wasteland is the *grizzled skipper*. A conspicuous little butterfly with attractive brown and white speckled wings, it is seen often quite early in the year from April to June, flying with fast wing-beats in a swift, darting flight pattern. It likes to bask in the sun with wings wide open, but as soon as the sun is hidden by cloud it closes its wings firmly shut and then becomes quite difficult to see. The eggs are laid singly on several plants used by the caterpillar for food, such as wild strawberry and silverweed as well as brambles. These caterpillars hatch in about ten days, and after feeding for about two months they spin cocoons with leaves and silk in which they pupate over the winter, emerging as butterflies in early spring. The butterflies live for only about two weeks. There is usually only one generation, but in hot years a second generation may hatch to fly in August.

Two more plants that grow on this sandy outcrop are parsley piert and subterranean clover. A member of the rose family, *parsley piert* is an inconspicuous plant that used to be widespread in our arable fields, but has declined sharply with the increased use of herbicides. Now it is more commonly found on sandy ground where the soil is thin. Only about 10 centimetres high, the stem of this plant branches extensively just above its base and bears leaves with three lobes that are deeply cut. The tiny stemless green flowers are borne in clusters and are well hidden amongst the leaves. The whole plant is delicately hairy and the flowers bloom from April to October. The word 'piert' is derived from the French name for the flower, *perce-pierre*, meaning 'break stone', indicating a plant that pushes its way through stony ground. Interestingly it was traditionally used to cure kidney stones.

The *subterranean clover* is a small clover that is difficult to find because of its creeping habit and small size. The stems are covered in soft hairs; the creamy white flowers are mostly infertile and the petals fall off early. What seed-pods do form have a curious habit of burying themselves in the earth when ripening; hence the plant's common name.

To the east of the path, just south of the railway line, is a stretch of soft marshy ground a few hundred metres long that 'quakes' if you jump on it. Be careful, though, because this is real bog you could find difficulty in getting out of. The underlying strata here are made up of impervious material such as gault clay, which acts as a trap for the water filtering through the chalk downs, so creating natural springs. Over time this formed the marshy peat bog which we find today. In June this is a magical place with an abundance of plant, animal and insect life. The bees hum loud, a wood pigeon calls in the distance 'coo-coo-coo-coo-coo', and the pheasant crows stridently nearby. The great variety of flowers here give much colour to this pleasant place, but sadly the distant noise of traffic and the sudden clatter of a train disturb its peace and tranquillity. Never mind, visit it and examine its natural history.

Plate 39 Greater Butterfly Orchid, Page 95 Author   Plate 40 Fragrant Orchid, Page 97   Author

Plate 41   Burnet Moth on 'The Pride of Sussex', Pages 52 and 98   Author

Plate 42   Elephant Hawk-Moth Caterpillar, Page 106   M. Hollings

Plate 43   Artefacts of Burlow Castle, Page 102   Author

Plate 44   Comma, Page 118   Author

Plate 45   Small Tortoishell, Page 118   Author

Plate 46   Stinkhorn Fungus, Page 119   Author   Plate 47   Spiked Rampion, Page 123   M. Hollings

Plate 48   Dryad's Saddle, Page 120   Author

Plate 49   Bluebells - Bramble Grove, Page 131   H. M. Proctor

Plate 50   Snowdrops, Page 141   Author

Plate 51   The Cuckmere before the reservoir 1968, Page 137   W. J. C. Murray

Plate 52   Mammoth Tusk uncovered 1969, Page 137   W. J. C. Murray

Plate 53   Coltsfoot, Page 140   W. J. C. Murray

Plate 54   Tuberous Pea, Page 141   Author

Plate 55   Elecampane, Page 141   Author

Plate 56   Wood Anemones, Page 131   Author

Plate 57   A Woodland floor in Spring, Page 131   Author

An uncommon flower, the *southern marsh orchid*, can sometimes be found here in profusion. This robust plant, which may reach 70 centimetres in height, has a large flowering spike carrying up to a hundred individual reddish-lilac blooms. These appear in mid-June and last until the end of July. The stem is hollow and soft, and the long yellow-green leaves are unspotted. *Common spotted orchids* with their spotted leaves also grow here, and to add to your confusion, hybrid species of both these orchids can be found.

Our way continues following the path eastwards until it crosses the railway and heads north towards Moors Hill. Just before Moors Hill the path descends into a small valley in which a small stream runs. Here you will see the *lesser water parsnip* growing. About a metre tall, this plant grows in wet places and has yellowish-green toothed leaves growing in pairs along the leaf stalk. The small white flowers are arranged in groups at the top of the stem and bloom from July to September.

As the path climbs up the hill, pause and look behind you at the view of Windover Hill and the Wilmington Giant. He stands out so magnificently, and I can so easily imagine him saying, 'Over here is the easy way to travel', remembering that in those far-off days the going where I stood was difficult indeed, covered as it was with trees, scrub and marsh.

Just to the right at the top of the hill is a small pond with many aquatic plants growing in and around it. A *crack willow* lies forlornly across one side of the road, its branches forming a mass of twisted growth over the water, a perfect nesting place for the pair of *moorhens* that live here. The crack willow differs from the other species of willow by lacking the covering or dense silky hairs on its leaves and by the peculiar brittle character of its twigs, which snap off with a cracking sound. *Water plantain*, *water forget-me-not*, and the *fine-leaved water dropwort* grow here. The latter plant has a stout, erect, hollow stem about a metre tall which grows out of the water and bears groups of small white flowers at its tips. The fine-leaved water dropwort flowers from June to September, but occasionally it can still be found in bloom as late as November. The lower leaves are almost hair-like and remain submerged in the water; the upper leaves are very finely cut and divided. This plant, closely examined or seen from a distance as it adorns the sides of this pond, has a beauty all of its own.

Sitting beside this pond with its own world of wildlife, one wonders what was its origin and what was its purpose? Look at the magnificent view across to the rolling downland hills and hollows from Windover Hill to Firle Beacon. This hilltop was probably close to early habitation and was almost certainly cleared for agriculture or livestock grazing fairly early on in human history. The pond could have been dug out of the Wealden clay to provide a store of water for animals or for humans. However, most probably they were formed by the digging out of marl which is a type of clay which was spread over sandy acid soils to improve their fertility and texture. You will find a number of these ponds, all with their own unique wildlife, scattered around the area, mostly on private ground.

Past the pond, the pathway soon forms a sunken trackway of Roman or perhaps pre-Roman origin. This is Farnestreet, referred to in 1220 as 'the old road' linking Pevensey and Lewes Castles. Now little remains of this road, which between about 1770 and 1830 was part of the main turnpike road from Lewes to Eastbourne via Hailsham and Polegate. We follow the road to the right as it turns sharply north-east before resuming its eastward direction past two lovely houses, Pickhams and Hayreed. In places the trackway runs through tunnels of overhanging shrubs, and at any time of the year there will be patches of damp, deeply rutted mud. The word 'Farnestreet' is probably derived from 'the way of ferns', and certainly its banks are covered with many lovely ferns. Ferns are among the most primitive plants on earth, and they date back more than 300 million years, when they were generally much larger than they are today. In fact the world's first forests were formed from tree ferns reaching 30 metres high, and these form the basis of our present-day coal deposits. Along Farnestreet grow large clumps of *hart's-tongue fern*. This fern has long, parallel-sided lime-green shiny leaves, and is abundant in woods on chalk-rich soils. Ferns are flowerless plants that reproduce by means of minute spores to be found in sacs on the underside of the leaf. The spores germinate and form both male and female organs, which fuse with the aid of moisture and develop into new young fern shoots.

Many lovely hedgerow plants grow on the banks amid the ferns, and in early spring primroses abound, soon to be followed by greater stitchwort. The lovely yellow *primrose* flower with its pale orange centre is so familiar to most people that little description is necessary. *Greater stitchwort*, however, may not be so familiar. This plant is one of the prettiest and most characteristic sights of spring, with its grass-like stem and leaves bearing numerous white flowers looking like the stars, from which it gets the Latin name *stellaria.* In places they are so numerous as to look from a distance like patches of snow gleaming in the early sunshine.

Badgers are common here, building their setts in the banks, and can easily be watched in the dusk.

Just about anywhere you will see one of our most widespread and commonest finches, the *linnet*. The male bird is dark brown in colour with a pinkish breast, and in the spring and early summer its breast turns crimson and it dons a crimson crown on the forepart of its head. The female linnet lacks the pink and crimson, and has a browner back with an overall more brownish-streaked appearance. The linnet can also be recognised by the undulating nature of its flight path and its twittering calls. The nest is built of roots, twigs and grass, lined with hair and feathers, at just about any height up to four metres in thorn bushes or gorse. The four to six whitish eggs, speckled with red and brown, are laid from April to June. As a young boy I remember a field just beside Farnestreet near Pickhams which was covered in gorse and brambles. I found many linnets' nests there as well as those of whitethroats, willow warblers and nightingales. Sadly, this wonderful field was 'grubbed out' for growing cereal crops in the late 1960s. Outside the breeding season the linnet, like most finches, is gregarious and is often seen feeding on weed seeds in large flocks. During the evening the birds return to the hedgerows to roost.

Heralding the arrival of spring is the call of the male *cuckoo*. Cuckoos arrive from Africa in April and May, returning in August. About 33 centimetres long, they have blue-grey plumage with white underparts and can be distinguished in flight by their pointed wings and long tails. They make no nest, but the female lays her eggs in the nest of other birds, such as the *meadow pipit*, *hedge sparrow* and *linnet*. She waits until her chosen host has completed laying and then lays one egg herself. The cuckoo's egg has a short incubation period and hatches out after only 12 days. The young cuckoo then instinctively pushes the host's eggs out of the nest and is reared by the foster parents until it leaves the nest after about three weeks. It migrates back to Africa alone in August or September, using an inborn navigational skill that is quite remarkable. I well remember finding many cuckoos' eggs in the nests of linnets breeding near Farnestreet. The eggs were easily distinguishable by their larger size and by being pale greyish-green spotted with darker markings of the same colour. The number of cuckoos arriving in Britain has certainly declined over the years, possibly because of droughts affecting their source of insect food over North Africa. However, it is most unlikely that you will fail to hear the cuckoo's unmistakeable and penetrating call while walking along this old Roman road in spring.

The hedgerows alongside Farnestreet in this area have been estimated as 900 years old, but because of the many changes that have taken place on this well-used route over the centuries they could be much older. *Oak* and *field maple* are common trees of these hedgerows, and what a magnificent sight they make in autumn when their golden leaves are silhouetted against the grey-blue sky and distant green of the Downs.

Carry on down Farnestreet past Hayreed and Thornwell and on to Robin Post Lane, where the next chapter starts.

10

ABBOT'S WOOD AND MILTON HIDE

Abbot's Wood is part of an extensive woodland that was once a large medieval forest called Lindhersse, an old Saxon name for the area. In the early part of the twelfth century it was owned by Battle Abbey but used by the monks of nearby Michelham Priory. Ditches and embankments still bear witness to the careful monastic husbandry of those times. It was transferred to the Duke of Devonshire after the dissolution of the monasteries in the sixteenth century. Finally, in 1953 it was sold to the Forestry Commission, who now manage it. Abbot's Wood itself is only about a quarter of the size of the forested area either side of Robin Post Lane. Other principal woods here include Wilmington Wood, Folkington Wood and Nate Wood, and for the purposes of this chapter all these woods are treated as one.

Milton Hide is an interesting area of acid heathland to the north-west of the forest, 200 metres or so either side of the lane between Hailsham and Upper Dicker. In Victorian times much of this area was an *osier willow* bed which was actively managed to produce pliant lengths of willow for making baskets and wattle fences. During World War II a landing strip was built across Milton Hide to provide rapid access for army troops stationed in the area. I understand from local people that only an Army Air Corps Auster ever used it, and then only occasionally. However, during its construction and when it was demolished in the 1950s, not enough care was taken to preserve the natural environment, and we lost the lovely *lily-of-the valley* plant mentioned as 'plentiful near Milton Hide' in A.H. Wolley-Dod's book *Flora of Sussex*.

On pre-World War II maps an area just to the east of Abbot's Wood itself showed up as unwooded, and indeed there were three open fields here known locally as 'The Tolls'. After the war these fields were planted with conifers, and when rides were constructed through them in the 1960s an ancient kiln was discovered and, nearby, a sunken pit containing many pieces of pottery. Evidence of this ancient industry can still be seen in the shape of deep depressions in the conifers to the south-east of Abbot's Wood.

The forest today is actively managed not only to provide timber but also to give the public an amenity for recreation. Many walks have been constructed, and the requirements of disabled people have been carefully provided for. The whole area is fairly flat, and walking and exploration is easy. Many species of trees can be seen in these woods, and little streams running in various directions give variety to the forest floor. A lake always existed in the middle of the forest, and on its southern side the remains of a medieval 'stew' pond can be seen today. A stew pond is a small area of water in which fish caught from the larger lake were placed to be kept alive until they were needed for cooking. The lake was much enlarged and improved after World War II by the construction of a dam and weir.

Coniferous trees such as spruce and Corsican pine predominate, but there are some good areas of oak, beech and birch interspersed with patches of chestnut and lime. Interesting trees worthy of special mention are the crab apple, hornbeam, red oak, spindle and wild service tree.

The parent of our cultivated apple tree, the *crab apple*, with its pinkish-white blossom, can be found in many places, especially in hedgerows at the forest edges. The name of this species is derived from the old Norse word *skrab*, meaning small rough tree. The crab apple seldom grows more than 10 metres tall, and lives for up to 50 years. Its leaves turn gold in autumn, and its small yellowish-green apples provide food in winter for birds such as fieldfares and redwings.

The *hornbeam* is quite common, and, with its smooth grey bark and oval leaves, can be mistaken for a beech. However, a closer inspection shows that its leaves are toothed and have bolder veins, and its trunk is always irregular, with wandering ribs running outside the main cylinder. 'Hornbeam' is a Saxon word meaning 'horny wooded tree'. Its wood is exceptionally hard, and it was pollarded for use as mallets, ox yokes and cogwheels for windmills and watermills. Today it is used for butchers' chopping blocks and for the moving parts of pianos. There is much evidence of pollarded hornbeam in Abbot's Wood and its surrounding area.

The *red oak* is a native of North America, but has been planted in many of our parks and woods. A fairly recent addition to Abbot's Wood, its leaves are much larger than that of our native sessile and pedunculate oaks, and its lobes are pointed, giving them a flame-like appearance, accentuated in autumn when they turn a vivid red.

Never more than five metres tall, the *spindle tree* is common along the wayside tracks in the forest, and can be recognised by the fact that its younger twigs are dark green and square in cross-section. The older stems become rounded with pale grey-brown bark, and its leaves, set alternately on the stem, are short-stalked, small and oval and have toothed edges. The small yellow-green flowers appear in May and are followed later by green fruit which turn a beautiful bright pink in autumn. These fruits gradually expand until they split into four, revealing four seeds covered in bright orange pulp. These contrasting colours soon attract birds that scatter the seeds far and wide. The spindle tree got its name from the fact that, because its wood was hard, smooth and kind to the fingers, it was used for centuries by womenfolk (known as spinsters) for spindles to spin wool. The wood is now used by gipsies to make clothes-pegs and skewers.

The uncommon *wild service tree* rarely exceeds about 13 metres in height, and is found only in a few of our ancient woodlands. In Abbot's Wood you can see a remaining example just south of the main car park, where it can be recognised by its grey bark. The bark of older trees is broken into squares and this gives it its Kentish name of *chequers tree*, since it looks like a draughts board. The leaves of this tree are about 5 to 10 centimetres long and 7 centimetres broad, oblong-shaped, with 6 to 10 oblong triangular lobes. The white flowers are formed in clusters and open in May. The small greenish-brown pear-shaped fruit ripen in November and have a pleasantly acid flavour.

Within these woods we find the normal complement of breeding birds, such as *sparrowhawks, warblers* of all kinds, and many of our common garden birds such as *thrushes, robins* and *wrens*. The *tawny owl*, too, is here, and this is one of our most familiar owls because of its characteristic deep call 'hoo-hoo-hoo', followed at an interval by a long 'oo-oo-oo-oo'. Another description of its call is the familiar 'tu-whit, to-whoo'. It is seldom seen in daylight except perhaps if hungry on dark winter days, when very occasionally it can be seen flying low over the woodland clearings looking for small rodents and insects. It nests in holes in hollow trees, favouring those covered with ivy. No nest material is used, and the four to six smooth white eggs are laid on decayed wood or the bird's own droppings as early as February or March. The parent birds are fiercely defensive of their nest, and particularly their young, and have been known to injure people who disturb them. Several pairs of tawny owls are resident in the area, and their nest sites are used by the same birds year after year. At times they will use the old nests of magpies, crows and hawks.

The *jay*, one of the most handsome of our birds, can be seen just about anywhere while walking through these woods. About 32 centimetres long, it is easily recognised by its pinkish body, white back and blue patch on its wing. The jay has a raucous call, 'scraak'. In spring this sound sends a chill through the smaller woodland birds, as the jay, like the magpie, does a great deal of harm to them by eating their eggs and young fledglings. Insects and grubs are their main source of food, however, and in the autumn they hoard acorns, like squirrels. These acorn hoards are sometimes forgotten and help to spread the oak when they germinate. The jay builds an untidy nest of sticks and roots, typically in a fork near the top of a young conifer, oak or sweet chestnut. The five to seven green eggs, spotted and freckled with light brown, are laid in April to June. Because of the secretive behaviour of the birds and the thick cover they frequent, the nest is particularly difficult to find. The birds can, however, be watched nest-building and when feeding their young.

The *goldcrest*, Britain's smallest bird, only nine centimetres long, is a fairly common resident breeding bird of the forest. Outside the breeding season it is often seen roaming around the trees with tits, giving out its distinguishing high-pitched shrill call of 'zee-zee-zee'. The small size of this bird distinguishes it from most others, but look out also for its plump form and prominent black, yellow and flame crest. The goldcrest builds a basket-like nest of moss, lichens, spider-webs and grass, all beautifully felted together and lined with feathers. The nest is suspended hammock-style about three metres off the ground from the branches of a coniferous tree. The seven to ten flesh-coloured eggs, spotted with brown, are laid from March to April, with a second brood in May and June. This second brood is often necessary to preserve this species, as many are killed off in a hard winter.

You may be lucky enough to see the *firecrest*, a bird similar to the goldcrest but much rarer. It can be distinguished from the goldcrest by its bold white stripe above the eye and black stripe through the eye. It is normally a winter visitor, but has started to breed in various places in southern England, although as far as I know not yet in or around Abbot's Wood.

You may catch a glimpse of the male *bullfinch*, which is a striking bird with its bright rose-red underparts and black cap. The female is duller, being pinkish-brown underneath, but retains the black cap. The bullfinch is quite common in the woodland, and in the spring its fluty call notes 'pew, pew' are often heard as it strips the buds off sloe and hawthorn bushes, its natural food. Watch out for the pure white patch above the tail as the bullfinch flies with an undulating flight pattern along hedgerows and woodland paths. It makes its nest in the lower branches of trees, usually evergreens, and in the tops of hedges and thickets about one to three metres off the ground. The nest consists of a platform of small twigs and fibrous roots in which is constructed a cup-shaped recess of finer roots lined with hair and a few feathers. Four to six greenish-blue eggs, spotted with dark purplish-brown, are laid from April to September.

Another bird you may encounter is the *crossbill*. A member of the finch family, this is a bird of the conifers and can be distinguished by its crossed bill and short, forked tail. The bill of this bird is specially adapted so that it can extract seeds from pine cones, and it can be seen feeding on the cones in a parrot-like fashion. The male crossbill has brick-red plumage with dark wings and tail, while the female is olive and yellow in colour. They breed regularly in Scotland, and as far as I know the crossbill does not breed in this area. Every few years or so large numbers of the bird arrive from the Continent in early spring. Look out for fallen, opened cones on the ground, as this will indicate their presence.

Autumn is the time to look out for yet another of the finch family, the *redpoll*. They are gregarious birds, and can often be seen arising from the bushes along Robin Post Lane with a characteristic 'buzzing' call, wheeling around before quietly settling again. They feed on weed seeds and are particularly fond of those belonging to the willowherb, which grows prolifically along the laneside. The redpoll is a small, streaked grey-brown bird with a bright red forehead. The male redpoll has a distinct pink breast. They are usually winter visitors to Sussex, but over the past decade have become increasingly adapted to our plantations of

117

conifer. They breed regularly in Scotland and North Wales, and are now well established in many parts of England. Perhaps it will soon be a regular nesting bird in the Abbot's Wood area.

Many of the butterflies I have described previously are to be found in Abbot's Wood: *orange tip*, *brimstone*, *speckled wood* and *red admiral*, to name but a few. When I roamed the woods as a boy in the early 1950s I found others such as the *white admiral*, *hairstreaks*, and *fritillaries*. These have become rarer, and in some cases are now absent altogether. Efforts are being made to re-create the open areas and rides which were common 40 years ago and in which these butterflies seem to thrive.

The *comma* can be seen basking in the sunshine just about anywhere from March on to early autumn. If you see an orange-brown butterfly with black markings and ragged edges to its wings, it is almost certainly a comma. So named because of the white comma-shaped markings on the undersides of its wings, this butterfly is an expert in camouflage. Not only do its caterpillars look like bird droppings, but when the butterfly rests with wings folded, the ragged edges and coloration of its wings makes it look just like a dead leaf. This allows it to remain undetected when the adult butterflies hibernate over winter amongst dead leaves. The eggs, looking like tiny gooseberries, are laid in groups on the upper side of hop leaves, nettles and currant bushes. The caterpillars feed for about seven weeks before pupating as a chrysalis for a further two weeks. Adult butterflies emerge in June to add to those already flying after hibernating in the winter. The comma tends to be solitary, and it lives in quite small areas of territory, favouring the nectar of such flowers as hemp agrimony, knapweeds and thistles. For reasons not fully understood, the comma population fluctuates. Thirty years ago they were rare, and now their numbers have increased markedly, so that it is a familiar and common sight not only in the countryside but also in urban gardens.

On Milton Hide on any sunny summer's day you will see many different species of butterfly. The *small tortoiseshell*, sometimes in large numbers, can be seen feeding on the blue flowers of the *devil's bit scabious* which covers the area. A very common butterfly, the small tortoiseshell hibernates over winter in garages and outhouses, and often enters houses to be found under pelmets and in curtains. As soon as the warm days arrive in spring, it flies out to join the brimstone as one of our earliest butterflies. The upper sides of its wings, some five centimetres across, are brightly speckled with orange, brown, black, yellow and blue markings, making it truly distinctive and beautiful. The underside of its wings are dull brown, giving it some camouflage when it rests with them folded. The eggs are laid in May, in groups, under nettles. The caterpillars are black with yellow stripes, and when they first hatch out they form a mass before eventually becoming solitary in their final stage. They feed on nettles for about three weeks and remain in chrysalis form for a further 12 days. The butterflies emerge in June and July and produce a further generation that fly in August and September and then hibernate. Often immigrants from France fly across the Channel in July and August to supplement the numbers already present. Strongly territorial, the small tortoiseshell will chase off any intruder that attempts to invade its favourite sunny patch.

Among the many moths to be found in Abbot's Wood is the black arches moth. The *black arches*, with a wingspan of four centimetres, is a striking black and white moth which looks like a bird dropping when seen resting on an oak tree in late summer. It gets its name from the wavy arched-shaped black lines across the upper surface of its wings.

One of the interesting puzzles of nature is why it is mostly male moths (and butterflies, for that matter) who spend hours sipping from dew or puddles of water. Recent scientific studies have revealed that they extract low concentrations of salt from the water during their process of sipping, so that they can transfer it to females during mating. This ensures that the eggs are endowed with a first dose of that valuable mineral, sodium. In the world of butterflies and moths the male is certainly worth his salt!

Autumn brings to the woods the usual array of fungi. One you are likely to smell before you see it is the *stinkhorn*. Well named because of its unpleasant odour of drains, this fungus first appears in early September as a rounded white object about four centimetres across, looking like an egg. When the 'egg' is ripe it ruptures, and within hours a spongy white tube 10 to 13 centimetres long emerges, carrying with it a dark green, slimy conical cap. This contains the mass of spores and is the origin of the smell, which attracts flies in their hundreds. They feed on the spores, and thus distribute them. When young and in its 'egg' form, this fungus is edible, but most people avoid it because of its smell.

The *oyster mushroom* is common, growing in large clusters on stumps or fallen trees. The cap, about 6 to 14 centimetres across, is often wavy and lobed and is deep bluish-grey at first, becoming paler and more fawn-coloured later. The surface is smooth and moist, and it has a pleasant smell and taste.

Many types of bracket fungi can be seen growing out of the wood of live trees as well as those that are dead. These fungi have small, crowded tubes below their cap instead of gills, and often form extensive patches with the brackets arranged in tiers along the tree trunk. Look out for the *many-zoned polypore*, with its distinctive cap with circular areas of grey, white and black. The colours are very variable, and some specimens can be found with colours ranging from black-green to grey-blue and brown. The tubes and pore surfaces are white and the flesh is very tough and leathery.

Another polypore called *dryad's saddle* can also be found growing on deciduous tree stumps, particularly of elm, beech or sycamore. It is easily recognised by the large and conspicuous fan-shaped fruit-body up to 50 centimetres across. This is coloured ochre-yellow and is ornamented with dark brown scales arranged roughly in concentric rings. This fungus causes a destructive white rot disease if present on living trees.

Visit Abbot's Wood very early on a morning in May or June. The dawn chorus has begun, a blackbird sings from the top of a bush with its deliberate loud and melodious warbling, a song thrush adds its musical phrases, and in the distant background a wren sings a long jingle of strident notes. It is so good to be alive as you make your way to the lake on the north-east side of the wood. As you near the lake a pair of *Canada geese* announce their presence with a harsh honking note, and a male *mallard duck*, with its glossy green head and purplish-brown breast, takes off from the water with a pattering of webbed feet along the surface. Sit here a while beside the weir, listen to the water as it trickles down to the brook below and gain an inner strength from the stillness of the trees.

Along forest walks and damp paths look out for *yellow pimpernel*. A neat, hairless plant with opposite oval-shaped leaves, yellow pimpernel trails along the ground and puts out solitary bright pale yellow five-petalled flowers. The flowers, which are just over one centimetre across, bloom from May to September. Just below the weir and along the stream you may also find a similar and related plant, *creeping jenny*. This differs from yellow pimpernel by having larger and more rounded leaves and bigger and brighter yellow flowers. The petals turn up to form a cup-shaped flower, whereas those of the yellow pimpernel are flat. Creeping jenny is also known as *moneywort* or *herb twopence* because of the shape of its leaves, which lie like two old pennies either side of its creeping stem.

Beside the lake grows the *skullcap*, which gets its name from the flower sheath which resembles a Roman soldier's leather skull-helmet. About 15 to 50 centimetres high, it has bright blue flowers less than two centimetres long, which appear in pairs from the stem at the leaf base. The leaves are lance-shaped and have smoothly rounded teeth. This plant favours wet places and can also be found on Milton Hide just north of the road. It flowers from July to September.

On badly neglected and overgrown tracks in moist shady places you may be lucky enough to find the *lesser skullcap*. It is closely related to the skullcap but is shorter, 5 to 20 centimetres tall, has smaller purplish-pink flowers, and its leaves are not toothed. I hope that with patience and good eyesight you will find both types of skullcap, which are not common and have a charm all of their own.

Before leaving the lakeside, I would like to recall how, many years ago, my love for classical music resulted from an experience I had beside its waters. It was late on a hot May afternoon, and a cold-weather front with towering cumulus clouds, like giant masses of cotton wool, was approaching. I could hear faintly the distant sound of thunder, but I decided to stay, as my bicycle was nearby under a tree and I had a cape in its saddlebag. The fall of water over the weir and the gentle hum of bees made this a delightful place; it became even more enchanting as the sound of a cuckoo penetrated the stillness from the direction of far-off Farnestreet. A breeze came up, clouds blocked out the sun and gradually it became darker. The first drops of rain pattered softly upon the lake. The birds fell silent, and soon thunder and lightning and great gusts of wind and rain swept through the trees. The storm soon passed, the song of birds returned and the trembling surface of the lake seemed alive as it glistened in the evening sunlight. This experience was truly rewarding, as some months later in a land far away over the seas I heard the sound of music emanating from a colleague's room. It immediately reminded me of the sounds of the passing storm that day beside the lake in Abbot's Wood. On further investigation, I discovered that the music was in fact that of Beethoven's 6th Symphony, the 'Pastoral'.

In the woods alongside Robin Post Lane grows one of our earliest flowering plants, the *butcher's broom*. This evergreen shrub is about 60 centimetres high and bears tiny greenish-white flowers from January to April and bright red berries from October to May. The flowers appear from the middle of the dark green 'leaves', which are not truly leaves but are in fact flattened branches each with a sharp spine at its tip. The true leaves are small thin scales at the base of these flattened branches. At one time butchers found that the prickly leaves were ideal for cleaning the tops of chopping blocks, and they were made into brooms for that purpose. It was also suspended in butchers' shops to keep away flies, which appear to dislike its smell.

On the western side of Robin Post Lane there are large areas where the wood has been cut down and 'harvested'. The ground is then 'grubbed' up and left as a wilderness of twisted and broken branches before they are replanted. These areas are exciting for the wealth of different plants that start growing with the increase in light from open skies. Look out for the *climbing corydalis*, an uncommon flower that has established itself in many of these places. It is a delicately constructed and graceful plant, with slender, brittle stems and much divided leaves which scramble over bushes and dead branches by means of tendrils. Up to a metre tall, it produces tiny creamy-white flowers from June to August, which form as little sprays growing out from the stem opposite a leaf. It seems to favour the damper banks beside hollows where water collects.

These wilderness areas are also favoured by such birds as the *willow warbler*, *chiffchaff* and *stonechat*. It is important that they are carefully managed so that, as they change character with the growth of new trees, new areas of a similar nature are created in the surrounding forest. This will ensure that the special wildlife of such habitats has a chance to survive.

In some of the remoter parts of the forest grows the *common cow-wheat*. This slender herb used to grow in large colonies all over the eastern side of the forest bordering the main road, but now it is confined to a few small areas in the north around Wilmington Wood. A parasitic plant, the common cow-wheat attaches itself to the roots of other plants, particularly the eyebright in this case, to get nourishment from them. It grows up to 60 centimetres high, with pairs of narrow leaves, from the base of which appear yellow or white flowers in June and July. Only bees, amongst the nectar-seeking insects, have the strength to prise open the closed lips of the flowers to obtain the nectar and effect pollination.

A number of our common plants have the prefix 'cow', and as a general rule it would appear to have been applied as a belittling term, as in the parallel cases of 'dog', 'horse' and 'hog', which signified worthlessness. However, in the case of cow-wheat, our forefathers perceived that the seeds, if ground up with wheat, would turn the flour black. Indeed, one now very rare variety, *field cow-wheat*, does have black seeds and was once a fairly common weed of the cornfield.

One rare and beautiful flower that can still be found along the woodland rides in June and July is the *spiked rampion*. Up to 80 centimetres high, it has a ribbed stem with a few slender, stalkless leaves. At its base are a number of larger oval heart-shaped leaves which have stalks and are toothed. The cream-coloured flowers form a large spike at the tip of the stems, and as the flowers open the spike elongates. The spiked rampion is declining fairly rapidly in Abbot's Wood, primarily because its habitat is being overgrown by brambles. Its striking flowers can be seen poking up through these brambles, but inevitably some cannot reach the light and therefore are not pollinated by insects. As this plant grows wild in only a few places in England, conservation efforts are required to protect and maintain its hold here in Abbot's Wood. A native plant of central and southern Europe, the spiked rampion was thought to have been brought to Michelham Priory by visiting monks for culinary purposes. Its root is thick and fleshy and is said to be very tasty when boiled and then mixed with olive oil, vinegar, salt and pepper.

All around you in the woods are many beautiful ferns. On the ancient parish boundary banks, *polypody ferns* grow with fronds up to 80 centimetres long. *Male fern*, characterised by its gracefully arching fronds, and *broad buckler fern* grow in places where the wood is damp and dark. Extracts taken from the roots of the male fern are used in homeopathy to treat septic wounds, ulcers and varicose veins. In ancient Greece these extracts were considered to be a valuable vermicide. Today they are used for expelling tapeworms, mainly by veterinary surgeons. Nearly all ferns reproduce by means of spores which appear from August to November as brown patches underneath the leaves. These are dispersed by wind and animals.

Before leaving the woods, mention must be made of the largest of our species of ant, the *wood ant*. This is very common in the woodlands, especially where pine trees predominate. Its large mound nests of pine needles, leaves and small twigs, up to a metre high, attract immediate attention. The nest is the home for up to 100,000 or more individuals, and their rustling as they move through the litter is often audible some distance away. Within the mound the ants construct galleries which connect up with a labyrinth of intercommunicating chambers beneath ground level. The hillock has entrances at different levels on the surface, and these are closed off with twigs at night and guarded by sentinel ants.

Wood ants feed on various types of insect, and they are particularly fond of aphids, which abound in the surrounding trees. They forage far and wide from their nests, forming straight and direct trackways which extend out up to 100 metres or more. Often you will see wood ants marching down these trackways, dragging dead insects many times their own weight, and they do a great deal of good work clearing the forest of insect pests. Each wood ant's nest contains numerous queens, some of which will emigrate with a number of worker ants to form new colonies. The wood ant has few enemies except the green woodpecker and Man, and its nests can remain occupied for 50 years or more. Do not disturb their nests, for not only do the ants have sharp mandibles with which to bite, but they also shoot out formic acid up to 30 centimetres' distance, which soon immobilises other insects and will give unpleasant sensations to the skin of humans.

On the acid heathland of Milton Hide *bracken* is found. This is perhaps the best known of our ferns, and it spreads by means of its underground roots as well as by the generation of spores. This heathland has a characteristic flora all of its own. Here you will find *ling* heather in profusion, together with such plants as devil's bit scabious, lousewort, petty whin and saw-wort.

Devil's bit scabious is a common plant on our heaths and damp grassland. The roots of this plant were once boiled in wine and used to treat snake-bite and many diseases, including the plague. They are short and come to an abrupt end, giving rise to the saying by ancient friars and monks that 'the root was longer until the devil bit away the rest from spite, envying its usefulness to mankind'. About 80 centimetres tall, the devil's bit scabious has deep blue flowers which form clustered round heads at the end of long stalks and bloom in July to October.

Wherever you find *lousewort* growing you can be sure that the soil is poor and lacking in nutrients. Lousewort was so named because our forefathers thought it produced the lice which infested sheep. However, the only connection between the plant and lice was the wet and poor pasture on which both thrived. Sheep were often grazed on poor land and the resultant lice infestation was incorrectly blamed on the plant. Lousewort is a semi-parasitic herb belonging to the same family as the common cow-wheat, and has a trailing stem with hairless much-divided feathery leaves and pink or reddish flowers. The flowers bloom continuously from April to August.

Petty whin is a small prickly shrub up to 30 centimetres tall with bright yellow blossoms which flower in May and June. The slender stems spread in all directions and are covered with small, pointed oval leaves. The stems are covered in long, slightly curved spines from which it gets its other name of *needle whin*.

Named after its saw-like leaves, *saw-wort* grows in damp places on Milton Hide. Up to about a metre tall, it has an erect leafy stem which bears a cluster of purple flowers looking like a small thistle, from July to September. The Latin name of this species, *tinctoria*, indicates that it is a dye weed, and indeed the leaves of saw-wort produce a greenish-yellow dye which was once used to colour wool.

To the east of Milton Hide, and also in the woodland, see if you can find *orpine*, a rare plant with large, flat fleshy leaves and purple flowers. The leaves contain a large store of water, and it has a root tuber rather like a carrot. The whole plant is some 50 centimetres high, and it is in flower from July to September.

An attractive willow, the *creeping willow*, grows on Milton Hide and is easily recognised by its reddish, wiry stems that creep through the grass at ground level. This shrub is fairly common locally in Sussex.

In this chapter we have examined many aspects of the natural history in the area around Abbot's Wood, but there is much else to see and study. You could spend many years tramping the paths of this delightful place and still you would only scratch the surface of the variety of wildlife to be found there. Whatever time of the year and wherever you walk in this area, you will find something to stir your emotions and create an interest. From the stillness of a cold frosty day in winter on the heathland to the cool, shadier woods in the heat of summer, you will not forget the places you have visited, the sounds you have heard, or the sunbeams and shadows of a remote woodland path.

Jay

Grey Wagtail

11

BRAMBLE GROVE AND MICHELHAM PRIORY

Bramble Grove is a small ancient wood situated just north of Milton Hide and just east of Michelham Priory. The wood itself is private, but a public footpath traverses the north side of it and the Wealdway passes close by. You can reach the wood either by the path that leads north-east from Milton Hide or by the Wealdway from Upper Dicker, which crosses the Cuckmere River just beside Michelham Priory. This latter path is interesting because it takes you past the entrance to the Priory moat and over an old bridge across a bypass stream of the main river.

Much has been written about Michelham Priory, and I do not wish to dwell on it at length here. Ever since the Priory was built, around 1229, for 13 Augustinian canons, this has been a place of peace and tranquillity and a haven for the wildlife that abound in the surrounding forests. Today, although open to the public and attracting many visitors, there is still an atmosphere of peace prevailing.

Wildfowl of many kinds inhabit the huge moat around the Priory, and a pair of *grey wagtails* frequent the stream just to the north. The largest of the three British wagtails, the grey wagtail is

127

recognised by its grey and white upper parts, primrose-yellow breast and rump, and long black tail. The male has a prominent black chin and throat in the summer months. It has an undulating flight pattern and calls with a metallic 'tseetsi'. The grey wagtail is a bird of the rocky streams in the hill country of northern Britain, but a few inhabit the remoter parts of some Sussex rivers. It is nice to see this very beautiful bird around the Cuckmere here, where it most probably breeds. Both parent birds build an attractive nest made of rootlets, grass and moss, lined with hair and a few feathers. It is situated, never far from water, in crevices, in rough and uneven banks and also in stone walls or under large boulders. The four or five greyish-white eggs with pale brown spots are laid in April, May or June. The nest is quite difficult to find, but when disturbed the sitting bird flies off and hovers with its mate, uttering noises of alarm. They can easily be watched back when building or when feeding young, but be careful you do not linger and unnecessarily disturb them, as they are commonly prone to desertion.

Along this part of the river, if you sit patiently on its bank you may see the *mink*. A friend of mine tells an interesting tale of mink seen on the moat, and I quote verbatim from her article in the parish magazine *Arlington Scene* of February 1992.

One sunny morning after a hard frost in mid-December, I took a stroll down to Michelham Priory, following the Wealdway from Upper Dicker. Reaching the bridge near the moat, I heard a scuffle in the bank to my right. I could just see something which looked like a tail wriggling furiously on the edge of the ice, but partly hidden by the shrubs. A moment later a black animal appeared, and I could see that it was attacking a very plump eel 12–18 inches long. The mink continued to bite the eel and chased it writhing and slithering across the ice to the other bank. The mink and eel disappeared from sight. The drama had not finished! Another smaller mink appeared on the right bank and swam under the ice, surfacing onto a concrete platform four feet in front of me. It stood on its haunches and stared at me, ran a few paces and stood up again. He did this three times, then lost interest, picked up a dead eel and swam back under the ice to the far bank. He (or she?) promptly killed another much smaller eel. No wonder mink are unpopular animals – three eels in 20 minutes, with no consideration for conservation through selective culling!

In fact, because of their increasing numbers and the danger they present to other wild creatures, mink are kept under control in the area by humane trapping.

A common and handsome plant growing beside the Cuckmere, here and in many other places along its length, is the *Indian balsam*. A native of the Himalayas and now completely naturalised on river banks throughout the country, it stands some two metres high, with thick, hollow, reddish stems. The leaves are large and deeply toothed and grow opposite each other on the stem. The hooded, pink and rose-coloured flowers some four centimetres long appear from July to September. Another, much rarer balsam, the *orange balsam*, has established itself in several places beside the Cuckmere. A native of eastern North America, this plant is much smaller than the Indian balsam, only about 50 centimetres high, and has smaller flowers, which are orange and bloom from June to August. Each flower has a long spur that bends back through 180 degrees at the tip. Look for this plant growing on the river bank where the bridge crosses the river next to the moat to the north of the Priory.

Before proceeding to explore Bramble Grove itself, let us pause awhile beside the bridge over this delightful river and ponder on what it was like when monks went about their work, unhurried by the ways of the world about them. I remember being here on a September day in 1995, after that great drought had turned what had been green fields brown, and the Cuckmere was but a mere trickle. The first rain for months had just fallen and one felt that autumn had just begun nibbling at the trailing edge of summer. *Willow warblers* were flitting about the alder trees, fattening up on insects before gathering together for their long flight south. A small *wren* sounded his alarm with a harsh churring, for this little bird delights to play the sentinel. Small *brown trout* could be seen hurriedly darting to and fro in the shallow water, hunting for snails and crustaceans. These fish are non-migratory and spawn eggs in winter along gravel banks washed by running water. There are plenty of such places along this stretch of the Cuckmere.

A short distance upstream is a weir that controls the flow of water to the moat and to the Cuckmere bypass stream. The water here, held back by the weir, is deep, black and still. Sit on the grassy bank and see the reflections of ferns, their intricately sculptured fronds seemingly etched for ever on the surface of the water. Male *midges* dance in the late summer sun awaiting autumn, when they will mate and then die. The female midge lays hundreds of eggs on the surface of the water in a mass of jelly, which then gets caught up on something solid. After hatching, the larvae swim freely before settling down onto the muddy bottom, where they feed on decaying plant material. Eventually, the larva climbs back out of the water, sheds its skin and after drying flies off as another midge.

Time to move on up the Wealdway, across a field and into Bramble Grove. This wood contains many different species of tree, but mainly *oak*, *hornbeam* and *sweet chestnut*. In a few places the uncommon *small-leaved lime* grows. As its name implies, this species differs from the common lime by having leaves only half the size, about five centimetres across. In winter, lime trees can be easily recognised by their buds set alternately along reddish somewhat zigzag twigs. The leaves, which open in late April, are heart-shaped with toothed edges and are very palatable when young. They can be eaten raw as salad and make tasty morsels for grazing sheep, rabbits or cattle. This fact probably explains why the lime, which was once a common tree in our oak woods some 5,000 years ago, is now truly native in only a few small isolated pockets. Linden is the old name for lime, and Lyndhurst in the New Forest of Hampshire literally means 'the wood of the lime trees'. However, any wild lime that tried to grow at Lyndhurst today would get short shrift from the New Forest ponies. So in medieval times the limes were almost eliminated from our woods simply by the pressure of grazing. Most of those we see today have been grown from stocks of Continental origin as ornamental trees for parklands and gardens, where their height, pleasing outline, grace and beauty and easy management are much in demand. However, the trees in Bramble Grove are most probably truly native and are the remnants of those that grew in much greater numbers in this ancient wildwood.

Lime flowers appear in May at the end of long stalks at the base of which grow wide, oblong modified leaves known as 'bracts'. Each flower has five yellowish-white petals and is highly fragrant and rich in nectar. They are favoured by bee-keepers for the amount of honey they yield. Lime flowers also are sometimes picked, dried and then used to make lime-blossom tea. Lime wood is pale yellow, soft, has an even grain and is a very good medium for woodcarving. The timber is also used for hat blocks which are carved by hand, and for fine joinery, including small boxes and frames for beehives. Lime bark is fibrous and countrymen formerly used strips from it for tying bundles, or made ropes by twisting them. So the lime tree has many uses, but sadly it plays no real part in the forester's plan today except as an addition to mixed woodland.

The time to view Bramble Grove at its finest is early April, when the exquisite white flowers of the *wood anemone* carpet the woodland floor before the first trees are in leaf. This is one of the earliest spring flowers to greet us in Bramble Grove. Its firm, fleshy roots creep just below the surface of the soil and then early in March they rapidly send up stems some 15 centimetres high, each with its whorl of deeply divided leaves just below the flower bud. The flower, some four centimetres across, has six to nine white floral leaves or sepals, which look like petals to the non-botanist. These sepals, which are sometimes delicately tinged with pink, enclose the male and female organs, which mature together so that self-fertilisation is made easy. Nevertheless, insects are still attracted to the fragrance of the flowers, and because there is no nectar for them on arrival they have to be content with just sucking the juices of the sepals. Each solitary blossom is a natural barometer, opening only when it is fine and remaining drooped and partly closed to protect the pollen when it is not. The stem, being firmly anchored to the ground, is so slender and pliable that it can easily withstand the strongest March gale as it bends with the wind. The flowers, too, are so shaped and hung that they turn their backs to the slightest wind. It is not surprising that it was called anemone or *windflower* after the Greek word *'anemos'*, meaning 'wind'. For weeks after the flowers have dried, the feathery leaves persist in building up food reserves in the roots for the following year, but as midsummer approaches they turn yellow and finally wither away.

No sooner have the wood anemones started to fade in Bramble Grove than they are replaced by another splendid flower of the spring, the *bluebell*. Bluebells store up a supply of food in their yellowish-white bulbs, buried deeply in the earth. These remain dormant during the summer and winter, but early in March long, narrow, deeply channelled leaves appear and push through, sometimes piercing the dead brown leaves that litter the ground. These first bluebell leaves gradually lengthen and turn a richer green, and soon at their centre what was once an empty tube fills up with a flower spike of closely pressed buds. This rapidly extends and soon the whole area of ground is filled with bluebell spikes, all pointed upwards amongst a sea of dark green leaves. A few premature plants show off their beautiful bell-shaped flowers of blue at a very early date, but it is not until spring is fully with us that the woodland floor is seemingly covered with a light blue mist; or, as the great poet Tennyson so aptly describes it, 'that seem the heavens upbreaking through the earth'. Bluebells increase so rapidly by forming new bulbs, and also from seed production, that they soon dominate large areas of woodland. Dense carpets of bluebells form, and with their masses of long leaves they effectively prevent colonisation by other plants. It is the leaves that are the key to its success, for it is they that grow large and become rich in sap; this eventually empties itself into the bulbs, which swell and divide themselves to produce new plants in the following spring. The flowers themselves are fertilised and then swell into green seed pods, which turn brown and eventually split open, revealing the numerous polished black seeds. In the woods of late summer, only the dry stems with brown seed pods still swaying in the wind remain to show what was once the glory here in spring.

On shady mossy banks at the edge of the wood, look out for the first of our orchids to bloom, the *early purple orchid*. One of our commonest orchids, it has been known for many years and was referred to by Shakespeare in *Hamlet* as 'long purples' and 'dead men's fingers'. These names clearly allude to the purple flower spikes and the curiously bloated tubers of this plant. As early as January, the first blunt dark green spotted leaves start to protrude above the moss, but it is not until late March that the flower spike begins to show. As the days lengthen and the sun gains in strength, so the stem lengthens and the leaves enlarge to form a large rosette at its base. Soon, about 6 to 30 reddish-purple flowers appear in a loose spike at the end of the stem about 40 centimetres high. The flowers each have a purple hood, a long, blunt spur which curves upwards and a lip that is as broad as its length, with small spots of darker purple. They bloom from April to June and have an unpleasant smell of cats, which becomes stronger after they have been open for some time. The early purple orchid is a good ancient-woodland indicator, and in Bramble Grove, as in most places, the numbers of flowering plants fluctuate markedly each year. Interestingly, this orchid also grows in open places on the Downs; possibly from the time they were heavily wooded. The tubers of this orchid were once thought to have aphrodisiac powers, and a breakfast drink known as 'salep' was prepared from them in the days before coffee became popular.

Many of our common birds nest in this small wood. Springtime is when they are most active, and one you will probably hear before you see it is the inconspicuous and somewhat secretive bird, the *dunnock* or *hedge sparrow*. It plaintively calls a high, piping 'cheep-cheep' from the top of a bush at the woodland edge.

Suddenly you see it as it drops to the ground and shuffles with slow gait, its wings flicking more or less continuously as it collects pieces of moss for its nest. A somewhat dull-looking bird, it has a brown back and wings with a steel-grey throat and chest. Its nest of moss and twigs, lined with hair, is placed about one or two metres off the ground in a bush, typically bramble, hawthorn or holly. The four to six eggs, of a beautifully marked, turquoise-blue colour, are laid from March to as late as July.

Here in Bramble Grove you are likely to encounter the *wren*, one of our smallest birds, just about anywhere, with its little plump brown body and short upturned tail. The wren has an amazingly loud, joyous song, and it seems incredible that such volume of sound heard can emanate from such a small throat. Wrens are common throughout Britain, and can be seen all the year round, hunting in the woods and copses for insects. They are very sensitive to cold weather and often huddle together on winter nights to keep warm. The cock wren will build several nests up to three metres off the ground in almost any nook or cranny, but especially in ivy growing on walls or up trees. The nest is domed, with an entrance only two centimetres in diameter, and is made of moss, grass and leaves. The hen bird chooses the nest in which to lay her eggs and lines it with feathers. Males sometimes have several mates, each of which lays between four and eight small white eggs sparingly spotted with reddish-brown. These are incubated by the female and hatch out after about 14 days. Both parents feed the nestlings, which fly after about 15 days. Between 1955 and 1957 in preparation for a college thesis, I made a careful study of occupied wrens' nests and was interested to discover that the entrances to 80 per cent of them faced east, i.e. in a direction away from the prevailing wind. The remaining 20 per cent facing west were occupied in early June (probably second broods) when the weather was warm. Instinct has certainly taught this bird some useful tips on how to keep warm.

Many of our common butterflies frequent the wood, including the *speckled wood* and *orange tip*. One to look out for is the lovely *peacock* butterfly, so named because the four large, brightly coloured eye-spots on its upper wing surfaces look just like those on a peacock's tail. These eye-spots scare away predatory birds; once the butterfly opens its wings, they do not stay around to investigate the origin of the large 'eyes'. The butterfly, when at rest, accentuates its eye-spots by rapidly opening and closing its wings, making a scraping noise as the wings rub together. The wingspan is some six centimetres, and with its rich colouring of purplish-red, blue, yellow and black, this butterfly can be considered one of our most striking. You will probably see it patrolling woodland paths or open sunny patches, where it chases away any intruder from its territory. The peacock hibernates in sheds and outhouses in autumn and winter, and is tempted out to feed on hazel catkins on warm spring days. The life cycle then starts again and the female lays batches of a hundred or more eggs under nettle leaves, which hatch out into hairy black caterpillars after about two weeks. These feed on the nettles for about 35 days and then turn into chrysalids, which hang down from the nettle stems on silken threads or from the trunks of nearby trees. The adults emerge in July and become a common sight in the countryside and in our gardens, feeding on buddleia and rotten fruit.

Early summer in Bramble Grove brings with it a profusion of wild flowers to replace the bluebells and wood anemones of spring. On the western edge of the wood there is a damp area, and here grows a familiar plant, the *ragged robin*. It is a very descriptive name for this plant, which bears unmistakeable rose-red flowers, each with five petals cut deeply into four lobes, giving them an overall 'ragged' appearance. The slender, reddish stem is about 60 centimetres tall, with lance-shaped leaves arranged in pairs along its length. Ragged robin is still called by its country name of *cuckoo flower* in some places, because its appearance coincides with the calling of the cuckoo. Its Latin name, *flos-cuculi*, also reflects this fact. Folklore associates plants with 'robin' in their name with goblins and evil, and it is still considered unlucky to pick this plant and take it indoors.

On the woodland margins and in hedgebanks you will find another red flower of the same family as ragged robin, the *red campion*. It differs from ragged robin by having much broader leaves and flowers whose petals are broader, have only two lobes, and do not have a 'ragged' appearance. Also its stems are green at the top, not reddish, and are covered all over with soft white hairs.

On shady parts of the woodland floor you will find the *yellow archangel* or *weasel snout*. Its specific Latin name, *galeobdolon*, derives from two Greek words meaning 'weasel' and 'stench'. These probably allude to the flower's upper lip looking in profile like part of a weasel's, and to the unpleasant smell produced if the leaves or stem are crushed between the fingers. The smell is said to deter plant-eating animals and insects. The plant is 30 to 60 centimetres high, with nettle-like leaves and handsome yellow two-lipped flowers blotched with brown. The flowers are carefully designed to allow only long-tongued bees access to the nectar at the base of the flower tube. A landing platform is provided by the lower lip, and the upper lip is so shaped that the sex organs within it brush pollen onto the back of the bee as it inserts its head into the flower. As it visits other flowers, so the pollen on the bee's back fertilises them. Other insects that are not large enough to touch the pollen are prevented from reaching the nectar by a ring of hairs inside the flower tube. The yellow archangel forms sheets of colour in the woodlands from April to June.

As the year progresses, the familiar *foxglove* plant begins to put up its tall straight stem with large downy leaves in open woodland glades where the soil is acid. The long, narrow spike, one to two metres tall, carries a succession of large, drooping, tubular pinkish-purple flowers which cannot be mistaken for any other wild plant. Bees love them, and if you sit down in front of a foxglove you will see each bee methodically working its way up the stem, visiting just about every flower that is open. Foxglove flowers first open low down on the stem in May and progressively appear higher and higher up the stem until September. The whole plant is highly poisonous, but the drug digitalis, used for treating certain heart ailments, is made from its dried leaves.

Although spring and early summer is the best time to see the wild flowers and birds of this ancient wood, you should also take the opportunity to visit it when the leaves change colour and begin to fall. Blackberries are ripening on the many brambles that cover the woodland floor, and on the edges *blackthorn* shrubs are covered with blue berries, each with its characteristic white waxy hue. These berries are called sloes, and when sugar is mixed with their pulp a tasty jelly is formed. When gin is added to this, and the resultant mixture is left to settle awhile before straining, a rich liqueur called sloe gin is produced. This autumnal harvest of fruit is relished by the blackbirds and thrushes, who are the first to taste them to be followed later by a great influx of fieldfares and redwings that soon relieve the bushes of all their glowing colours.

The wood is now a mass of colour, and with the first November frosts and the first chill winds of winter the leaves begin to fall. Each slight breath of air brings down an inconceivable multitude of green and yellow, gold and bronze, brown and crimson. It would seem that all the trees would soon be denuded to the very last twig, but the following day yet another draught of frosty air brings with it a further twinkling shower of leaves. Soon the floor is seemingly covered with a brown carpet, giving warmth and shelter to many small creatures which must endure the biting cold of the months to come. Winter comes quickly, and the trees look gaunt and naked as their branches stretch skywards. Only the hornbeam keeps a slight covering of faded pale-brown leaves all through the winter cold.

Soon the new year arrives, and the first leaves of the many spring flowers begin to appear through the dead leaf litter to begin again the wonderful cycle of nature.

12

ARLINGTON RESERVOIR

In the mid 1960s Eastbourne Water Company (now part of South East Water) realised that the underground chalk streams which had supplied water to Eastbourne and the surrounding district for many years would not be able to cope with the increasing demand for water supplies to new housing developments and for industrial expansion. An ambitious plan to dam the Cuckmere River at Arlington was devised, to create a reservoir with an area of 49 hectares (120 acres) containing 3,545 megalitres (780 million gallons) of water. This Cuckmere River scheme was authorised in 1968, and permission was given to build the reservoir and treatment works and to abstract up to 45 megalitres (10 million gallons) of water a day from the river, but at the same time ensuring that a minimum flow down the river was maintained. Construction work started in 1968 and was completed in 1971.

The reservoir was formed by cutting off a meander of the Cuckmere with a concrete-faced earth dam just to the west of Arlington. During excavations several interesting animal remains were found, including a mammoth tusk, a bison horn and the skull of a woolly rhinoceros dating from 250,000 years ago. Roman pottery, too, was found at Polhill's Farm, indicating that this was an important industry here in Roman times. Before construction work commenced, this area was one of great natural beauty, with many wild plants and breeding birds. Although some breeding birds, such as the snipe and redshank, have inevitably been lost, much, much more has been gained, thanks to the wisdom and foresight of South East Water.

The Reservoir and surrounding area is now a Nature Reserve and a Site of Special Scientific Interest (SSSI) controlled and actively managed by South East Water. Over 30,000 native trees have been planted, including *oak, birch, wild cherry, hazel, whitebeam, rowan* and *hawthorn*. The land on the north side of the water, once bare and uninteresting, is now a wonderful area of scrub and young trees, ideal for nesting *nightingales, whitethroats, finches* and *tits*. A hide for birdwatching has been constructed here as well as an osprey nesting platform. In addition, for over 24 years the Reservoir has been used as a trout fishery. This is managed by South East Water for about 250 members who fly fish for *rainbow trout*. These members are often keen naturalists themselves and help to record and update information on the wildlife of the area.

Some areas, especially on the southern shoreline, are left unmown to encourage a wide variety of tall grasses and wild flowers which attract many kinds of butterflies and moths. *Clouded yellows* can be seen here in late May and June, and the rare *pale clouded yellow* has also been recorded. *Marbled whites* and *skippers* are common, and a few of the rare *white-letter hairstreaks* seem to have established themselves in a small area beside the Reservoir. Of the many plants of this natural grassland, special mention must be made of the *common spotted orchid* which is beginning to spread and establish itself.

Arlington Reservoir has been designated an SSSI for the amount of wildfowl that inhabit it over the winter period. More than one per cent of the United Kingdom population of wintering *widgeon* duck are to be found here, and a total of 176 different species of birds have been recorded to date. Some of these are exotic and very rare, and include the *Slavonian grebe, black tern, little stint* and *red-rumped swallow*. Who knows what will turn up in the future?

Ospreys are regularly seen fishing over the Reservoir in spring, and in 1992 an artificial nesting platform was built on the north shore to encourage this wonderful bird of prey to nest in the area. In April 1995 great excitement was caused when no less than three ospreys were seen catching fish from the Reservoir and using the platform as a perch on which to dismember and eat their catch. This bird of prey always used to nest in trees or ruins on islands amongst the lonely lochs of the Highlands of Scotland. However, they were vulnerable to human predation, and the last pair bred at Loch Archaig in 1908. It was about 1955 before they returned to Scotland (Speyside) to re-establish themselves as a breeding species, and now, as everyone knows, they nest in many places in the Highlands. I well remember my first sight of this magnificent bird when on a climbing holiday in the Cairngorms in late April 1955. I saw it hovering over a grey and misty Loch Morlich and then plunge head first, near vertically, to catch a fish. It was easily recognised by its white head and gleaming white underparts. As I write now, 40 years later, there are plans to reintroduce the osprey as a breeding species somewhere in England. It would appear that all an osprey requires is plenty of fish and a suitable area of large trees in which it can build its huge nest of sticks, moss and grass. With Abbot's Wood and Friston Forest nearby, and a well-stocked reservoir, wouldn't it be remarkable if the publication of this book coincided with the first recorded nesting of the osprey in Sussex, or indeed in England!

The area around Arlington Reservoir is quiet and peaceful, with many walks leading off to interesting places. The Wealdway passes close by, and this is well worth following northwards to Sessingham Moat; and there are undisturbed and secluded stretches of the river partly hidden by overhanging *alder*, *willow* and *blackthorn*. Sessingham was mentioned in the *Domesday Book*, when it housed a population of over 50 and had a watermill. The river was obviously important, as reference was also made to dues of 500 eels imposed on the settlement. An ancient trackway leads from Sessingham eastwards across the river to Tye Hill. On the slopes of this hill, at the far side of the field to the north of the track, is a raised bank, and this marks the southern boundary of a medieval deer park of about four square kilometres. This bank can still be traced in a number of places in the area south of Michelham Priory, and when it was used to contain wild deer it would have been topped by a wooden fence.

Walk past Tye Hill on a crisp and clear January day when the naked trees stand up starkly as black and somewhat sinister sentinels against the low sun over the dark Downs. In the hedgerows see the dome-shaped mass of twigs of an old magpie's nest that will be used again in April. The river at the bridge is full and muddied as it sweeps boldly down to the pumping station at the Reservoir. From here it will be pumped up to ensure a full dam of water ready for any dry summer. You will see *redwings* and *fieldfares*, and *long-tailed tits* which will entertain you as they flit through the blackthorn bushes. Little patches of golden brown attract your eye beside the track where sheltered oaks have kept their covering of leaves; but for how long, you ask yourself, as you feel the wind rising and see the first storms of midwinter approach, heralded by the sun setting behind golden cirrus and sombre black nimbostratus clouds.

In your walks around Arlington Reservoir look out for the *barn owl*, a few pairs of which still nest in the area. This owl has generally decreased over the years, perhaps owing to changes in land use, disturbance and pesticides. It is closely associated with man and is attracted to farm buildings, church towers and ruins, which provide suitable dark places in which it can nest or roost. From these bases the barn owl will go out to hunt for rodents, small birds, frogs and insects. Indigestible parts of the food, such as bones, feathers and fur, are regurgitated as pellets, and these are often found near to places where these birds roost and nest. Although normally nocturnal, the barn owl may be seen quite frequently hunting by day, especially on winter afternoons when food is scarce or on summer evenings when its young require large amounts of food. You will not mistake this attractive and intelligent bird with its large white facial discs, orange-buff upper parts and pure white underparts. The small black eyes face forwards, giving them binocular vision and the ability to judge distances with precision. The disadvantages of having forward-looking eyes is overcome by the bird having the ability to swivel its head around through 180 degrees. On still nights you may hear their long, wild shrieks as they call to each other. They make no nest, but two to six pure-white eggs are laid in April or May on spaces under roofs, in rock crevices or in a hole in really big old trees. After about a month the eggs hatch out into comic-looking little baby owls covered in soft white down. When hungry or disturbed they utter strange sounds like high-pitched snoring. The young owls are fed by both parents for about two or three months, until they are strong enough to fly off on their own. I hope you will get the opportunity to see the barn owl's graceful, silent form as it glides over the green fields in the dying evening light. I know that great efforts are being made to provide the correct environment, and particularly nesting sites, for this attractive bird; in the end only man has the power to destroy or preserve it.

As the earth tilts and the northern hemisphere warms, bringing with it the first signs of spring, so you will see a blaze of golden-yellow flowers growing in places beside the Reservoir. This is *coltsfoot*, which is fairly common on waste ground and banks where the soil is poor and heavy. It has vigorous, creeping underground stems called rhizomes, from which emerge, as soon as the last frosts have gone, scaly stems each bearing a flower head nearly three centimetres across. The flowers appear in February or

March, well before the large leaves – as much as 20 centimetres across – start growing. These leaves, which last through the summer, are covered with white cottony down underneath, and their shape gives the plant its English name of coltsfoot. When dried they were once used for tinder to light fires, and they were also smoked as 'tobacco' to give relief from coughs. The Romans prized coltsfoot, and used it to relieve asthma and bronchitis as well as coughs. Even today the rhizomes are still boiled in sugar, and the resultant 'coltsfoot rock' is used to soothe sore throats. In Paris, coltsfoot flowers were often painted on the doorposts of apothecaries' shops as a sign. Its Latin name, *tussilago*, derives from the word 'tussis', meaning a cough. Indeed, Lowland Scots still call the plant *tussilugi* and use it as a cough relief.

Another harbinger of spring is the *snowdrop* which can be found growing in profusion along the roadsides and paths around Arlington and indeed just about everywhere in the Cuckmere Valley. This beautiful flower is one of the first to attract the early bees to its honeyed groves of green set within its pure white bell-shaped blossoms poised on slender stalks. Sometimes called 'the fair maids of February', what pleasure they give as they pierce through a late winter fall of snow and harmonise with their surroundings.

Some interesting and uncommon plants grow beside the road from Berwick to Upper Dicker. Here, just to the south-west of Arlington Reservoir, grows the attractive *tuberous pea*. It is also known as the *Fyfield pea*, because it grows commonly in fields about Fyfield, Essex. This pea has a creeping rootstock from which small edible and nourishing tubers grow. The angled stem trails over the ground and climbs surrounding bushes up to two metres or so high. Along the stem are leaves made up of egg-shaped leaflets and tendrils. The bright crimson flowers are borne in loose clusters of two to six at the end of long stalks. They are wonderfully scented and bloom from June to August. At Arlington the flowers are easily seen growing over the roadside hedges; but, as I write in 1995, they seem to have disappeared from beside the road opposite the entrance to the Reservoir. However, they will probably reappear, and in any case they are well established within the grounds of the Reservoir itself.

To the south of Berwick Station, on the road towards Berwick village, and protected by conservation posts, are two more uncommon plants, *elecampane* and *spiny rest-harrow*. Elecampane is not a truly native plant, but was probably introduced from the Continent by the Romans. Growing up to almost two metres high, with large saw-toothed leaves and velvet underneath, it bears heads of yellow flowers some eight centimetres across. Flowering in July and August, it can be seen growing in the ditch beside the road. It has been known there for many years; how it got there nobody knows, but it was once widely cultivated as it was prized for medicinal purposes. People would use it for chest infections and take it in syrup form for coughs, asthma and bronchitis, whilst the roots were used for cleansing the kidneys. The Romans used to cut the root into small pieces and eat them as we would a dish of peanuts. In Elizabethan times the roots were candied and used as sweetmeats. The elecampane is closely related to the *common fleabane*, a much smaller plant which grows in damp places just about everywhere.

On the opposite side of the road is a patch of wasteland where you will find a fine colony of *spiny rest-harrow*. Growing up to 60 centimetres tall, this member of the pea family has erect spiny stems from which grow pink flowers from June to September. The spiny rest-harrow thrives on rough grassland, especially on heavy clay soils. Its close relative the *common rest-harrow*, which is similar in appearance, is fonder of calcareous soils near the sea, and has a tough underground root system which used to delay the passage of horse-drawn ploughs or harrows; hence its name. When the leaves of either rest-harrow are eaten by cattle, the resultant milk becomes tainted with an unpleasant goat-like smell. This is particularly pronounced when turned into cheese, and such cheese is called 'cammocky'. This smell is most apparent when the leaves are rubbed and crushed together in the fingers. In Sussex and Hampshire one of the local names for rest-harrow is *cammock*. In ancient times the young leaves of rest-harrow were preserved in vinegar and used as a pleasant sauce to be eaten with meat. A liquid extract of its flowers and roots was also used by herbalists to treat disorders of the urinary tract.

Before the last war the *otter* was a widespread and fairly common mammal on rivers and streams throughout the country. Even up to the early 1950s otters were often seen on the Cuckmere River around Arlington. One person who has lived by the river all his life told me how otters were found dead on the railway track near the crossing above Sherman Bridge. They were electrocuted as they tried to cross the live line, and he used to skin them and sell their pelts.

Otter numbers sadly declined in the late 1950s because of hunting and trapping by water bailiffs along salmon and trout rivers. Now, thanks to a more enlightened attitude to hunting and trapping, the otter is again increasing in numbers. It is spreading eastwards from its stronghold in the West Country and westwards from East Anglia, where it is being released into the wild following a successful captive-breeding programme. I have spoken with somebody who is familiar with the otter in the wild, and he convinced me that he saw one feeding on an eel beside the river, near to the Reservoir. Another reliable source told me that he had recently seen otter tracks on a muddy bank just above Arlington. I have no reason to doubt that remnants from the original otter population still exist in quiet places here. Certainly the river is well stocked with the otter's favourite food: eels and fish.

The otter grows to a length of about 80 centimetres, and has a beautiful streamlined body covered in a close-fitting chocolate-brown fur which is waterproof. Its throat is lighter in colour, and with a long (up to 50 centimetres) tapering tail and webbed feet it is well suited to swim and dive in the water. The otter's nest, or 'holt', as it is called, is merely a hole in the river bank, or a tunnel amongst tree roots. Frequently one of the entrances to the holt is beneath the water level. Two to four cubs are born each year, seemingly in any month, and there is probably only one litter per year. Both parents look after their cubs well, but as soon as the young can take care of themselves, the male, or 'dog', otter leaves the family to live on his own. The bitch continues to live with the young until she mates again.

The otter is solitary and secretive by nature, and is not often seen by day. The best indication of its presence is by its webbed tracks in the mud or by its droppings, called 'spraints'. The otter's tracks are distinctive: large and padded, with five-pointed toe marks. They are often followed by the drag mark of its tail. The otter's spraint is left in selected places to warn other otters of a territory already occupied. Spraints are usually deposited on top of large stones under a bridge or other shelter where they are unlikely to be destroyed by wind, rain or sun. I hope that you will find these signs showing that the otter is indeed present on the Cuckmere. South East Water are providing a suitable habitat for this beautiful mammal by maintaining an unpolluted river and ensuring that its banks are natural and not unnecessarily cleared or cut back. Let us hope that the otter continues to live undisturbed here by this delightful river and that its numbers will increase.

I hope this brief description of the Reservoir and its surrounding area will tempt you to visit it. A wealth of natural history awaits you, and even if you just come to its shores on a cold, dark, depressing day in the depths of winter, you will still be rewarded by the sight of hundreds of waterfowl and other birds.

At the end of your wanderings let the Yew Tree Inn nearby in the ancient village of Arlington give you sustenance and a warm welcome.

Osprey

EPILOGUE

I have taken you on a journey up the Cuckmere Valley and described areas of interest that are rich in natural history. You will have seen the river emptying itself into the sea over the pebbles on the Haven shore, and you will have looked down from High-and-Over and viewed the river as a gleaming ribbon of blue set upon a carpet of green as it meanders gently southwards. From the top of Windover Hill you will have looked down the valley to the distant sparkling sea and felt the voiceless wind as it sweeps over the rolling Downs. In quiet corners near Arlington you will have felt the extraordinary rhythm of the river as it flows slowly through the tranquil glades coloured by the countless flowers that thrive in these damp and shady places.

I hope that not only will you have visited places previously unknown to you, but that you will also have absorbed some of their beauty and developed an interest in their wildlife. Clearly I have only scratched the surface of the rich natural environment of the valley. Much has been left out, but my objective will have been achieved if your interest has been aroused and natural history becomes an absorbing pastime.

From the short description of adders and glow-worms you will have gained an insight into how cruel nature can be. Your thoughts may then have started to turn to the philosophy of life.

Why are we here and who made the world as it is? Wordsworth, a great lover of nature himself, touched on this subject, and the moral and philosophical lessons to be learned from life, when he wrote in his poem *Tintern Abbey*:

> ...with an eye made quiet by the power
> Of harmony, and the deep power of joy,
> We see into the life of things.

And later, in the same poem:

> ...And I have felt
> A presence that disturbs me with the joy
> Of elevated thoughts; a sense sublime
> Of something far more deeply interfused,
> Whose dwelling is the light of setting suns,
> And the round ocean and the living air,
> A motion and a spirit that impels
> All thinking things, all objects of all thought,
> And rolls through all things. Therefore am I still
> A lover of the meadows and the woods,
> And mountains; and of all that we behold
> From this green earth; of all the mighty world
> Of eye and ear...

We must never forget that we, as human beings, are different, not only mentally but also physically, from the rest of the animal kingdom. For we have the power to think for ourselves, to make logical deductions and to act decisively in a sensible manner; quite unlike animals, who rely almost entirely on instinct. With such gifts we must seek to preserve our natural heritage. Throughout this book you will have noticed how important plants were, and still are, in the treatment of many kinds of medical disorders. We lose these plants through extinction at our peril, for who knows when some species might be crucial to our survival?

The trend towards more and more subsidies encouraging farmers to convert marginal land into productive crops must be reversed. Over the years we have lost too many of our wildlife habitats to intensive farming. Increasing field sizes, resulting in fewer hedges, has led to a marked reduction in birds like the partridge and corn bunting. Pressure must be applied to European governments to change agricultural policies so that farmers are actually discouraged from having large fields and encouraged to

146

put more land back to nature. The 'set-aside' scheme is a step in that direction, but much more must be done.

I hope you have enjoyed the book not only as something of interest to read but also as a useful guide to the natural history of a beautiful part of our country.

By chance I came across a poem by an unknown author contained in a booklet written by my grandfather ('Young Warren') and published in 1942. With a slight adaptation it sums up for me the spirit of this delightful river.

Though I may range in foreign lands,
Beyond a dreary sea,
The home I leave in England
Shall still be dear to me.
And as the river seeks the sea
My thoughts to it shall flow,
To muse on scenes I dearly loved
In the days of long ago.
For wheresoever my path shall lead,
And whatsoever befall,
I'll ne'er forget the hills and Downs,
The Cuckmere and its call.

ACKNOWLEDGEMENTS

Nobody could compile a book such as this without a good deal of help from others. Many have contributed directly, others I have spoken to only on the telephone. Some have walked the ground with me and experienced the emotions described. I thank you all, but particularly I wish to thank Helen Proctor and Dennis Vinall for their proof-reading and helpful and constructive comments on the script, to say nothing of their photographs contained herein. Also my thanks to Michael Hollings for permission to include some of his wonderful collection of wildlife photographs. My thanks also to the Arlington Village Hall for the loan of the late W.J.C. Murray's photographs for inclusion in this book. Others to whom I am indebted are Edward Batt, Peter Battrick (National Trust), Simon Buller, David Candlin, Peter Davys, Cyril Fuller (Forestry Commission), Alan Gardner, Michael Hartt (South East Water), Dr Rodney Johnson, Helen Jones, Roy Neeve (Butterfly Conservation), Bob Piper, Glen Redman (National Trust), Peter Sexton, Janet Simes, The Reverend Peter Williams, Commander Peter Winter, DSC, RN, and Phil Wooller.

I am particularly indebted to my friend Frank Wootton, OBE, for his wonderful paintings, landscape drawings and bird sketches. These, together with the illustrations by Sue Davies, speak for themselves and I thank them both for their important contribution.

This book probably would not have been written without the generous support of South East Water, who from the beginning gave financial assistance, and to them I am deeply grateful.

Finally, my warm thanks to Walter Clark for his hard work and patience in typing the script from illegible handwriting.

BIBLIOGRAPHY

AA Book of the British Countryside, Drive Publications, 1973.

Birds, Trees and Flowers, Odhams Press, 1947.

Brown, Leslie, *British Birds of Prey*, Collins, 1976.

Campbell, Bruce, *Finding Nests*, Collins, 1953.

Doff, Elizabeth, *Discovering the Cuckmere*, 1992.

Evans, A.A., *A Saunterer in Sussex*, Methuen, 1935.

Fisher, James, *The Fulmar*, Collins, 1952.

Harrison, David, *Along the South Downs*, Butler and Tanner, 1958.

Kearton, Richard, *British Birds' Nests*, Cassell, 1908.

Lang, David, *Orchids of Britain*, Oxford University Press, 1980.

McCarthy, Edna and Mac, *The Cuckmere*, Lindel Publishing, 1981.

* Martin, W. Keble, *The Concise British Flora in Colour*, Rainbird, 1965, 1969.

Murray, Walter J.C., *Copsford*, R. and W. Clark, 1948.

Nicholson, E.M., *Birds and Men*, Collins, 1951.

* Perring, Franklyn, and Walters, Max, *British Wildflowers*, Macmillan, 1989.

* Peterson, Roger, Mountford, Guy, and Hollom, P.A.D., *A Field Guide to the Birds of Britain and Europe*, Collins, 1954.

* Phillips, Roger, *Mushrooms and Other Fungi of Great Britain and Europe*, New Interlitho, 1981.

* Reader's Digest, *Field Guide to the Butterflies and Other Insects of Britain*, 1984.

Step, Edward, *Wayside and Woodland Blossoms*, Frederick Warne, 1941.

Sussex Wildlife Trust, *A Vision for the South Downs*, 1993.

Walley, Paul, *Butterfly Watching*, Severn House Naturalist's Library, 1980.

Wickham, Cynthia, *Common Plants as Natural Remedies*, Frederick Muller, 1981.

Wolley-Dod, A.H., *Flora of Sussex*, The Chatford House Press, 1970.

* These are useful books for identification purposes.

LATIN NAMES OF FLOWERING PLANTS

autumn lady's-tresses — *Spiranthes spiralis*

basil thyme — *Acinos arvensis*
bee orchid — *Ophrys apifera*
bell heather — *Erica cinerea*
bird's nest orchid — *Neottia nidus-avis*
black nightshade — *Solanum nigrum*
bluebell — *Endymion non-scriptus*
branched bur-reed — *Sparganium erectum*
bristly ox-tongue — *Picris echioides*
broad-leaved helleborine — *Epipactis helleborine*
brooklime — *Veronica beccabunga*
buck's-horn plantain — *Plantago coronopus*
burnet rose — *Rosa pimpinellifolia*
butcher's broom — *Ruscus aculeatus*

calamint — *Calamintha ascendens*
carline thistle — *Carlina vulgaris*
celery-leaved buttercup — *Ranunculus sceleratus*
chicory — *Cichorium intybus*
climbing corydalis — *Corydalis claviculata*
clustered bellflower — *Campanula glomerata*
coltsfoot — *Tussilago farfara*
common bird's-foot trefoil — *Lotus corniculatus*
common centaury — *Centaurium erythraea*
common cow-wheat — *Melampyrum pratense*
common fleabane — *Pulicaria dysenterica*
common rest-harrow — *Ononis repens*
common rockrose — *Helianthemum nummularium*
common spotted orchid — *Dactylorhiza fuchsii*
common twayblade — *Listera ovata*
cowslip — *Primula veris*
creeping jenny — *Lysimachia nummularia*
creeping cinquefoil — *Potentilla reptans*
crosswort — *Cruciata ciliata*

deadly nightshade — *Atropa belladonna*
devil's bit scabious — *Succisa pratensis*
dog rose — *Rosa canina*

dog violet	*Viola canina*
dwarf centaury	*Centaurium capitatum*
dwarf orchid	*Orchis ustulata*
early forget-me-not	*Myosotis ramosissima*
early purple orchid	*Orchis mascula*
early spider orchid	*Ophrys sphegodes*
elecampane	*Inula helenium*
evening primrose	*Oenothera biennis*
eyebright	*Euphrasia nemorosa*
felwort	*Gentianella amarella*
field cow-wheat	*Melampyrum arvense*
field pansy	*Viola arvensis*
field scabious	*Knautia arvensis*
fine-leaved water dropwort	*Oenanthe aquatica*
flowering rush	*Butomus umbellatus*
foxglove	*Digitalis purpurea*
fragrant orchid	*Gymnadenia conopsea*
frogbit	*Hydrocharis morsus-ranae*
frog orchid	*Coeloglossum viride*
fyfield pea	*Lathyrus tuberosus*
glasswort	*Salicornia perennis*
golden dock	*Rumex maritimus*
greater butterfly orchid	*Platanthera chlorantha*
greater knapweed	*Centaurea scabiosa*
greater sea spurrey	*Spergularia media*
greater stitchwort	*Stellaria holostea*
great hairy willowherb	*Epilobium hirsutum*
great mullein	*Verbascum thapsus*
ground thistle	*Cirsium acaule*
hairy violet	*Viola hirta*
hemp agrimony	*Eupatorium cannabinum*
henbane	*Hyoscyamus niger*
honeysuckle	*Lonicera periclymenum*
horseshoe vetch	*Hippocrepis comosa*
hound's-tongue	*Cynoglossum germanicum*
indian balsam	*Impatiens glandulifera*
jack-by-the-hedge	*Alliaria petiolata*
kidney vetch	*Anthyllis vulneraria*
lady's bedstraw	*Galium verum*
lady's smock	*Cardamine pratensis*
lesser burdock	*Arctium minus*
lesser sea spurrey	*Spergularia marina*

154

lesser skullcap	*Scutellaria minor*
lesser spearwort	*Ranunculus flammula*
lesser water parsnip	*Berula erecta*
lily-of-the-valley	*Convallaria majalis*
ling	*Calluna vulgaris*
lousewort	*Pedicularis sylvatica*
marsh mallow	*Althaea officinalis*
marsh marigold	*Caltha palustris*
marsh woundwort	*Stachys palustris*
milk thistle	*Silybum marianum*
moon carrot	*Seseli libanotis*
mountain stone parsley	*Seseli libanotis*
musk thistle	*Carduus nutans*
narrow-leaved bird's-foot trefoil	*Lotus tenuis*
orange balsam	*Impatiens capensis*
orpine	*Sedum telephium*
parsley piert	*Aphanes arvensis*
petty whin	*Genista anglica*
pheasant's eye	*Adonis annua*
ploughman's spikenard	*Inula conyza*
primrose	*Primula vulgaris*
purple loosestrife	*Lythrum salicaria*
pyramidal orchid	*Anacamptis pyramidalis*
ragged robin	*Lychnis flos-cuculi*
red bartsia	*Odontites verna*
red campion	*Silene dioica*
red helleborine	*Cephalanthera rubra*
red poppy	*Papaver rhoeas*
red valerian	*Centranthus ruber*
reedmace	*Typha latifolia*
rock samphire	*Crithmum maritimum*
round-headed rampion	*Phyteuma tenerum*
sainfoin	*Onobrychis viciifolia*
saw-wort	*Serratula tinctoria*
sea aster	*Aster tripolium*
sea beet	*Beta vulgaris*
sea couch grass	*Elymus pycnanthus*
sea holly	*Eryngium maritimum*
sea kale	*Crambe maritima*
sea lavender, rock	*Limonium binervosum*
sea pink	*Armeria maritima*
sea purslane	*Atriplex portulacoides*

scentless mayweed	*Tripleurospermum maritimum*
sheep's sorrel	*Rumex acetosella*
silverweed	*Potentilla anserina*
skullcap	*Scutellaria galericulata*
smooth hawksbeard	*Crepis capillaris*
snowdrop	*Galanthus nivalis*
southern marsh orchid	*Dactylorhiza praetermissa*
spiked rampion	*Phyteuma spicatum*
spiny rest-harrow	*Ononis spinosa*
spring whitlow-grass	*Erophila verna*
squinancy wort	*Asperula cynanchica*
star thistle	*Centaurea calcitrapa*
storksbill	*Erodium cicutarium*
stonecrop	*Sedum acre*
strawberry-headed clover	*Trifolium frangiferum*
subterranean clover	*Trifolium subterraneum*
sweet violet	*Viola odorata*
sword-leaved helleborine	*Cephalanthera longifolia*
thrift	*Armeria maritima*
tormentil	*Potentilla erecta*
traveller's joy	*Clematis vitalba*
tuberous pea	*Lathyrus tuberosus*
viper's bugloss	*Echium vulgare*
wall germander	*Teucrium chamaedrys*
water crowfoot	*Ranunculus peltatus*
water forget-me-not	*Myosotis scorpioides*
water pepper	*Polygonum hydropiper*
water plantain	*Alisma plantago-aquatica*
weld	*Reseda luteola*
white helleborine	*Cephalanthera damasonium*
white horehound	*Marrubium vulgare*
wild clary	*Salvia horminoides*
wild clematis	*Clematis vitalba*
wild mignonette	*Reseda lutea*
wild pink	*Dianthus plumarius*
wild strawberry	*Potentilla vesca*
wild thyme	*Thymus drucei*
wood anemone	*Anemone nemorosa*
wood sage	*Teucrium scorodonia*
woody nightshade	*Solanum dulcamara*
yellow archangel	*Lamiastrum galeobdolon*
yellow bird's-nest	*Monotropa hypopitys*
yellow horned-poppy	*Glaucium flavum*
yellow pimpernel	*Lysimachia nemorum*

yellow rattle	*Rhinanthus minor*
yellow toadflax	*Linaria vulgaris*
yellow vetch	*Vicia lutea*
yellow vetchling	*Lathyrus aphaca*
yellow water lily	*Nuphar lutea*
yellow-wort	*Blackstonia perfoliata*

INDEX

Bold numbers refer to plate numbers. Main reference pages are in bold italics.

159

INDEX

Musk thistle *84*
Mute swan *105*
Mycorrhiza *23*, 40
Myxomatosis 7, 46, 90, 91

Narrow-leaved bird's-foot trefoil *14*
Nate Wood 113
National Trust 7, 73, 77
Needle whin *125*
Neolithic people *2*, 5, 87
Nettle plant 49, 118, 119, 134
Newt 54
Newt great crested *41*
Nightjar *47–48*
Nightingale *48*, 111, 138
Nodding thistle *84*
Norman period *6* 101

Oak 112, 114, 115, 119, 130, 138
Old man's beard *33*, *84*
Orange balsam *129*
Orange tip *95*, 118, 133
Orchid, autumn ladies tresses *97*
Orchid, bee *30*, *70–71*
Orchid, bird's nest *40*
Orchid, broad-leaved helleborine *40*
Orchid, common spotted *97*, *109*, 138
Orchid, common twayblade *96*
Orchid, dwarf *83*
Orchid, early purple *132*
Orchid, early spider *23–24*
Orchid, fragrant *40*, *97*
Orchid, frog *54*
Orchid, greater butterfly *39*, *95–96*
Orchid, marsh 102, *109*
Orchid, pyramidal *36*, *37*, *83*
Orchid, red helleborine 43
Orchid, southern marsh *109*
Orchid, sword-leaved helleborine 43
Orchid, white helleborine *21*, *39–40*
Orpine *125*
Osier willow *113*
Osprey 32, *138–139*
Otter *142–143*
Owl, barn *140*
Owl, long-eared *35–36*
Owl, tawny *115–116*
Oystercatcher 12
Oyster mushroom *119*

Painted lady *18*, *12*, 38

Palaeolithic age *1*
Pale clouded yellow 138
Parasol mushroom *29*, *56*
Parsley piert *108*
Partridge, common *77–78*
Peacock butterfly 38, *133–134*
Pedunculate oak 115
Peewit *19*
Peregrine falcon *11*, 36
Periwinkle 94
Petty whin 124, *125*
Pevensey , 5, 6, 110
Pheasant *76–77*, 108
Pheasant's eye *24*, *38*
Pickhams 110, 111
Pine 32, 114
Ploughman's spikenard *37–38*
Plums and Custard 42
Pochard 18
Polhill's Farm 4, 137
Polypody fern *123*
Pony 46, 136
Poppy, red 57
Poppy, yellow horned *13*
Pride of Sussex *41*, *98*
Primrose *110*
Privet 22, 102
Puffball *42*
Purple loosetrife *106*
Pyrite nodules 10
Pyramidal orchid *36*, *37*, *83*

Queen Mag *102*

Rabbit 7, 16, 46, *64*, 65, 78, 90, 91, 104, 130
Ragged robin *134*
Rainbow trout 138
Rat 12, 19
Red admiral *26*, *27*, 38, *49*, 118
Red bartsia *53*
Red campion *134*
Red helleborine 43
Red kite *32*
Red oak 114, *115*
Redpoll *117–118*
Red poppy 57
Red-rumped swallow 138
Redshank *19*, 102, 137
Red valerian *13–14*
Redwing *90*, 114, 135

163